T0196473

SELF-ESTEEM MATTERS

52 WAYS IN 52 WEEKS
TO
ENHANCE SELF-ESTEEM

Other Books by the Author

Archetypes, Unmasking your true self (Balboa Press, 2017)
Decoding the Afterlife (Possumwood Publishing, 2015)
The Queen (Possumwood Publishing, 2017)
The Knight (Possumwood Publishing, 2017)

Fiction

Tilly and the Magic Potion (Possumwood Publishing, 2013)
Charlie the Cheeky Spider (Possumwood Publishing, 2018)

SELF-ESTEEM MATTERS

52 ways in 52 weeks to enhance self-esteem

Brian Dale

Illustrated by Brian Dale

BALBOA.
PRESS
A DIVISION OF HAY HOUSE

Balboa Press books may be ordered through booksellers or by contacting:

Balboa Press
A Division of Hay House
1663 Liberty Drive
Bloomington, IN 47403
www.balboapress.com.au
1 (877) 407-4847

Print information available on the last page.

ISBN: 978-1-5043-1363-6 (sc)
ISBN: 978-1-5043-1364-3 (e)

Balboa Press rev. date: 07/10/2018

Dedication

This book is dedicated to my dear friend, Nicole Chapman-Picker.

It was her inquisitive mind and incisive questions that inspired me to extend my archetype knowledge into the role played by our self-esteem, that is, our Victim archetype.

Our personal self-esteem is so important. It dictates all that we do in life. It feeds our unfulfilled potential and inspires our passion and achievement.

To Nicole and all my readers, may your self-esteem be strong and resilient, to push you through all of life's challenges and give you the courage and inspiration to achieve greatness.

Self-Esteem Matters

❖ Self-esteem is the backbone of our personality.
❖ Self-esteem influences everything that we do in our life.
❖ Self-esteem is never static.
❖ Self-esteem changes with our life's experiences.
❖ To achieve, we need a strong self-esteem.
❖ To work through the challenges, we need a strong self-esteem.
❖ To be ourselves, we need a strong self-esteem.

So, how do we achieve and maintain a strong self-esteem?

We change our self-esteem by being vigilant and conscious of what we think, say and do. We consciously change our negative patterns of behaviour to positive patterns of behaviour.

As our patterns of behaviour change from negative to positive, our attitude and self-esteem strengthens. We grow in confidence. Our fears diminish and we enhance our ability to meet new challenges. As we recognize and credit our small achievements, they grow in number and importance. Each achievement builds upon the previous one. Each success empowers us and provides us with the incentive and strength of attitude to tackle larger challenges. Achievement and a strong self-esteem empower each other. As our self-esteem strengthens, our achievements grow in number and importance. This, in turn, strengthens our self-esteem.

A positive pattern of behaviour is established through a time frame of awareness and change. As we become aware of our negative patterns of behaviour and change to positive patterns of behaviour, our self-esteem flourishes.

Self-Esteem

Self-esteem is an attitude. Self-esteem is not an emotion.

Our personal self-esteem determines how we think, how we communicate and what we do in all of our life's experiences.

Our self-esteem determines what we think about ourselves.

Our self-esteem determines how and what we communicate to others.

Our self-esteem determines what we do and how we react to each different event in our life.

We come into this life with a pre-determined self-esteem. Our early childhood experiences weaken or strengthen our self-esteem. As we go through life, the events that we experience and how we react to those events weaken or strengthen our self-esteem.

Remember it is how we react to events not just the events themselves that either diminish or enhance our self-esteem.

An event that is generally viewed as negative, such as a personal health crisis can diminish or enhance our self-esteem. The individual can wallow in self-pity and wonder why an illness can strike them down and badly affect so many other things in their life. Alternatively, the individual can work through the illness with courage and endurance, change their lifestyle to a healthier model and re-direct their energy into more suitable activities.

Then, an event that is generally viewed as positive, such as a promotion at work, also has the potential to diminish or enhance our self-esteem. The extra pay and recognition is likely to enhance self-esteem. However, the promotion may also mean extra hours at work, working with new people, in a new situation and with added responsibilities and accountability which may diminish self-esteem.

When we have a strong self-esteem and a positive attitude, we can work through any obstacles and achieve both personal and social milestones.

Using This Program

This program is designed to strengthen your personal self-esteem.

There are 52 topics.

Each topic analyses the why and how method of improving your self-esteem. Each topic also has a set of exercises designed to improve your self-esteem.

The program is set out so that every week there is a new topic and a new set of exercises.

You may follow the program as it is designed.

Every day for week 1, keep the topic in your focus and practice the exercises. "Welcome the new day" is the topic for week 1. For each day of that week, keep your focus on that concept and practice the 3 exercises.

Then, every day for week 2, keep the "be grateful for your life" topic in your focus and practice that set of exercises.

Continue, every day for week 3 with your focus on that topic and put into place those exercises.

As the weeks go by, you will find that many of the exercises and activities you have completed will continue automatically, even though they may not be part of that week's program. That is great. You may even do them automatically already. That is perfect.

By the end of 52 weeks many of your archetypal behaviour patterns will change from negative to positive or your positive behaviour patterns will strengthen. Your self-esteem will grow stronger. Your attitude to yourself and what you think, say and do will broaden and grow stronger.

You may use the program to suit your own needs.

This program is designed for flexibility. If you do not wish to follow the program on a week to week basis, that is acceptable. You are free to pick and choose topics and exercises.

If there are certain negatives in your life that you wish to change or if there are certain strengths you wish to enhance then you may wish to pick and choose only several of the topics and exercises.

That is perfectly acceptable.

You may also wish to concentrate on a particular topic and exercise program for more than a week.

That, too, is perfectly acceptable.

This program is designed to suit your individual needs. Use the program on a week by week basis or pick and choose. The choice is yours. The aim is to strengthen and enhance your self-esteem. The aim is to enjoy life to the fullest and make the most of your talents.

Enjoy!

Week 1

Welcome the New Day

When you first wake up, take in the new day. Spend a few seconds or a few minutes absorbing what Mother Nature has to offer.

If you reside in a warm climate or, if it is the height of summer, observe and feel what is on offer. Enjoy the warming rays of the sun. Feel the warmth in the air. Breathe deeply and allow this warmth to penetrate your body. This is our sun, the sun that gives us life every single day.

If you reside in a cold climate or, if it is the depth of winter, take time to wonder at your surroundings. Feel the chill in the air. Look out your window and marvel at the frost, the fog, the snow and any other aspects that winter has to offer.

If you reside in a temperate climate and it is the middle of autumn or the time of spring observe the changes that are taking place. Are the trees losing their leaves or bursting with new growth? Is the wind rushing through the trees and causing the branches to wave vigorously or is it blowing gently and allowing the branches to sway peacefully?

Understand that you have been granted more time. You have been given another day. No matter what your commitments or challenges, your joys or blessings you have the choice of how you welcome this new day. You can welcome it with dread, fear, loathing or disinterest.

Better to welcome it with wonder, expectation, joy, peace and gratitude.

Week 1

Exercises

1. When you wake up or rise from your bed allow the light to penetrate your body. Breathe in gently and imagine the light filling your whole being.

2. Focus on an activity that fills you with happiness and joy.

3. Think or say quietly to yourself, "I have been given another day to be me."

Week 2

Be Grateful for your Life

You are alive, so it is time to make the most of your life.

Your life may be full of challenges or it may be full of joy. More than likely it will be full of both challenges and joy. That is the nature of life.

Even if you are struggling with the situation you have found yourself in always be aware that nothing is static and that everything changes.

If you feel you are living a charmed life, enjoy the moment. However, always be aware that nothing is static and there may be a challenge just around the corner.

Welcome the challenges as a natural part of life. Always look for the positive from even the toughest and most demanding ordeal. Learn the lessons that come from these challenges.

Just as importantly, welcome the joys and the good things that life has to offer. Enjoy them, each and every moment. When those times fill your life, cherish them with relish and enthusiasm. These times may be a small event, such as a comforting hug from a friend. They may also be a life-changing moment such as a monetary windfall or meeting the love of your life.

Always look for the positive in all and any situation. Life is to be lived. Live in the present and plan for the future. Make the most of your life as each opportunity will not come again.

Give thanks that you are alive. You have chosen to experience this physical plane and you have the power to honour that commitment with grace, purpose and gratitude.

Week 2

Exercises

1. Lie or stand quietly and focus on your physical body.

2. Feel your heart beat and give thanks that you are alive.

3. Focus on your mind and be in wonder of your ability to think and reason.

4. Use your imagination to go to your favourite place. Wonder at the magic of your imagination.

5. Feel the joy in your heart and understand that you can choose to feel that way no matter what.

Week 3

Give Thanks for What you Have

Focus and give thanks for what you have.

It is easy and convenient to think and talk about all the things that we do not have or all the things that we would like to have.

It is easy and convenient to compare ourselves and our life with others who we consider are better off or more fortunate. We are surrounded with media that compares and presents images that are deemed ideal. They are the false idols of our present civilization.

We all have personality traits that can enhance our life and the lives of others. We have the ability to be positive, friendly, empathetic, full of joy, accepting, encouraging, thoughtful and kind. We also have the ability to be the opposite. We can be negative, exclusive, angry, jealous, spiteful, rude and nasty. The choice is ours to make, each day and with every thought, word and deed.

We all have talents that can bring joy, achievement and prosperity. We may be creative, entrepreneurial, practical, intuitive, knowledgeable, possess physical prowess or mental toughness.

We are all presented with opportunities that we can use for the benefit of ourselves and others. Alternatively, we can totally ignore these opportunities.

Think about what you have. Consider your individual strengths and abilities and what you can do. Look at ways to improve yourself, your skills and your situation, yet always be grateful for what you have now and in the present and what you can achieve now and in the present.

Week 3

Exercises

1. Look around your living quarters and focus on something that you treasure. Smile!

2. Extend this thought to other things that you value.

3. Give thanks for all the wonderful people in your life.

Week 4

List all the Good Things about You

MY BEST QUALITIES

I am kind.

Resilience is my greatest strength.

My passion is caring for my family.

I love to garden.

My garden is amazing.

I have a great singing voice.

I care about all creatures.

My friends enjoy my company.

I love making teddy bears.

I am generous.

I always remember birthdays.

My house is unique.

I am loyal and faithful.

I never hold grudges.

This should be done with pen and paper. If you use a notepad or a small book, that would be ideal.

In a quiet moment and in a quiet space sit down and begin to write a list of all your good qualities.

You may list what you consider to be minor things, such as your smile, your hair, the way you converse on the phone. You may list what you consider to be major attributes such as your ability to repair machines, build houses, play sport, be efficient at work or be a nurturing and caring parent.

Take your time with this exercise. Think about each of these qualities. Think about the times when you put these qualities into practice and to good use. Think about other occasions when you could also put these qualities into good use.

Be aware that this list is not a comprehensive list. This is only the beginning. Every time you think of another positive aspect about yourself, add it to your list. This is your focus for the week.

This is no time to be self-effacing. This is a time to embrace all the good things about you even if you have trouble accepting some of those qualities. Think about the good and positive things others have said about you. Add them to your list.

Over time, expect this list to grow. Keep your pad or book nearby. Life is about experience, change and growth.

Week 4

Exercises

1. Buy a special book or note pad.

2. Allow yourself some quiet time and write down your good qualities.

3. Meditate or sit quietly and consider all those things that you have written down.

4. Picture yourself using one of those qualities and take in the emotion. How do you feel?

5. If you have the time, picture yourself using another quality and take in the emotion. You may choose to do this for each day of the week.

6. Keep your special book or notebook with you and jot down other special qualities when they come to mind. New qualities may come to you after you have completed a task, done something challenging or achieved a goal.

Week 5

Compliment Yourself on a Job Well Done

Now is the time for compliments.

When you have completed a task, done something worthwhile, reached a milestone or achieved a goal give yourself credit.

It does not matter how small or insignificant you consider your achievement to be. Give yourself a compliment. It does not matter how small or insignificant other people consider your achievement to be. The response is the same. Give yourself a compliment.

You may have just finished washing the dishes. Compliment yourself, "That was a job well done."

You may have just finished exercising. Compliment yourself, "I am pleased with my exercise regime. I am fitter and healthier than ever before."

If you have achieved a major milestone then celebrate in style and with an activity that you enjoy.

Be sensible with your celebration. Enjoy your achievement, enjoy your celebration and look forward to the next step in that process or area of your life.

Compliments are important. If you cannot compliment yourself, then, there is a good chance that you will not expect or accept compliments given by others.

Be proud and happy with your achievements and reward yourself with a compliment.

Week 5

Exercises

1. Give yourself compliments.

2. Begin by giving yourself compliments after you complete something simple that you do on a regular basis. It may be making the bed, cooking the evening meal, shopping, getting the children off to school; just something that may be considered trivial but which is very important.

3. Extend your compliments to all areas of your life; at home, at work, on holidays, at recreation and wherever you may be.

4. With some of your compliments, literally give yourself a pat on the back.

5. With each compliment, remember to smile.

Week 6

Giving and Receiving Compliments

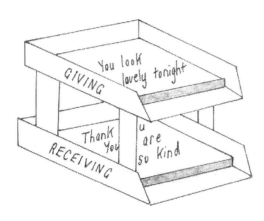

Compliments are vital to one's well-being and for increasing one's self-esteem.

How you accept a compliment is important.

When others pay you a compliment, please do not brush it away or fob it off. Always accept a compliment with joy and humility. If someone says, "That looks nice on you." Your response should be to smile and say, "Thank you."

If you can respond with a genuine compliment to the other party, then do so.

If you have ingrained the previous week's exercise into your behaviour you will then confirm the compliment by thinking or saying quietly to yourself, "Yes, I do look nice in this outfit."

When the occasion arises, compliment others. Always be genuine with your compliments. You do not need to make something up just to please the other person or for the sake of this exercise. Always be sincere.

If your compliment is brushed aside or fobbed off, then that is the end of the matter. There is no need to repeat the compliment or feel offended if you felt it wasn't accepted how you wanted it to be; too bad. How others accept compliments is not under your control.

Remember, like many things in life, compliments are to be given freely and with no expectation. Compliments are never to be used as a bribe.

Give and accept compliments with unconditional joy and humility.

Week 6

Exercises

1. If someone gives you a compliment say, "thank you" and smile.

2. Where possible return the compliment.

3. When the occasion arises, compliment others. The compliment must be genuine. Never feel disappointed with another's reaction to your compliment. You give compliments freely and without expectation.

4. Compliments you can use: "You look nice today." "Your hair looks great." "That outfit really suits you." "That was well done." "You are so good at this." "Well said." "I love how you do that." "It's great to have a friend like you." "I'm always happy when you're here." "You are so good with your children."

Week 7

Receiving Help and Assisting Others

We all need a helping hand at some time or other.

To some, receiving and accepting a helping hand will be a more important issue than receiving and accepting compliments.

However, both should be treated in the same manner.

We cannot do everything ourselves. There is nothing wrong with accepting assistance. It has nothing to do with being too proud or being too needy.

If another person or group offers assistance, then accept their help with joy and humility. We live in a society and social interaction is important for the health and well-being of both the individual and the society.

Never let pride interfere with your well-being.

If you need assistance, then ask for it. Always remember there are only two responses available, yes or no. Your response should be the same to either answer. You accept either answer with joy and humility.

If you have the time, energy, knowledge or resources to help others then do so. We all have that freedom of choice. We can choose to assist others or choose to ignore others.

Remember assistance should be given and accepted freely and without condition.

This is so important to remember when you offer assistance to others.

Week 7

Exercises

1. Make a list of all the things that you need assistance with. They may be small or large in nature. That does not matter.

2. On a regular basis ask a family member, friend, or association to assist you with one of those chores. If the job is done, give thanks and perhaps a small token of your appreciation, depending upon your relationship. If the request is denied, accept the response without any emotional attachment.

3. Every day this week, text, message or ring a family member, friend or acquaintance. Ask how they are going and if they need any help. You can say you were just thinking about them. Ask are they well and do they need any assistance.

Week 8

Yes or No

For just about every single question that we ask or that is asked of us, there are only two answers, yes or no.

There are so many occasions when we tread lightly around our answers or we spend an incredible amount of time justifying our response.

Why?

The answer to this question is our self-esteem. There are times when we feel that our self-esteem is under attack. In order to protect our composure we agree to something we really don't want to do or we make excuses.

Remember, from now on, there are only two answers, yes or no. If you agree, the answer is yes. If you disagree the answer is no.

"No" is one of the most difficult words to say.

When you respond in the negative, always remain polite but be firm. For example, "No, I don't want to come out tonight, I have other things to do."

When you get, "Come on, you'll have a good time." "What have you got to do that's more important?" "I need you to come with me."

Your response is, "No thanks." There is no need for further justification.

If you really feel the need to justify your answer, then be honest. You can be honest and gentle at the same time.

Practice your response with yes or no. If you have to, add one single reason.

Week 8

Exercises

1. When you are home, going for a walk, driving in your car, exercising, taking a bath or any other activity when you are alone say out loud, "no, thank you." Say it with a smile.

2. After you have practiced saying, "No, thank you" you may add one reason. "No, thank you, I am too busy." "No, thank you, I am happy to stay home this evening." "No, thank you, it's not the sort of thing I go to." "No, I don't lend money but thanks for thinking of me." "No, I'm not drinking tonight but it's alright that you do."

3. Find at least one occasion where you politely say no.

Week 9

No Argument, No Discussion

There is nothing wrong with a robust discussion. We all have an opinion and on many occasions we are free to express that opinion. Free and open discussion is an important aspect of human interaction.

However, there are situations when there is not a free and open discussion but a forcing of one person's desire onto another.

Consider the times when you have been forced into agreeing to a request. These are not the times when genuine compromise has taken place but rather an occasion when you have been physically, emotionally, psychologically or financially coerced or even bullied into something that you didn't agree with or didn't want to do.

How do you stand in your own power?

The answer is a simple technique that needs a lot of practice.

You state your response and state one reason only. You do this calmly and firmly but with no emotion.

When the other party or parties begin the process of discussion, argument, opinion, consequences, emotional blackmail, threats and all kinds of psychological games you remain firm.

You state your response and your reason once again. You do not enter into the argument or the discussion. You do not justify your position. You stay calm and resolute.

Remember, practice makes perfect. If you do not wish to do something then the answer is "no" with no argument and no discussion.

Week 9

Exercises

1. This is a difficult exercise to practice without the co-operation of another person. So, find a person willing to work with you. It may be your partner or a good friend. You are going to do some role-playing.

    Your partner or friend needs to play the devil's advocate. They will ask or demand that you do something. It doesn't really matter what the question or demand is. Here are some examples. "How about we go to the movies?" "Can you lend me some money?" "There's a better show on T.V. than this one." "I need your help now." "You're not wearing that are you?" "You'll have to do it, I'm too busy."

    Your part is to say, "No." Smile and give one reason why you are not going to agree with the request or demand.

    Your partner or friend needs to harass you a little with comments like "Why not?" "It will be fun." "You have to come." "Why are you acting like this?" "You are so negative." "Boy, are you grumpy." "Don't you like my company?"

    Your job is not to argue or justify. You may repeat your reason one more time and then end or change the conversation politely.

    Remember to end the conversation quickly. There is to be no argument, no discussion and no justification.

Week 10

Emotions

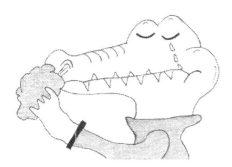

Always control your emotions and never let your emotions control you.

This never an easy task but it can be done.

We are human and we are emotional. You are not being asked to be robots and to never express your emotions.

What you are being asked to do is to control your emotions.

If you are involved in a dispute or disagreement, you need to stay calm and rational. As soon as you become angry, frustrated, teary, hysterical and the like, you cannot possibly represent yourself or your argument to the best of your ability.

If you need to express your anger then do so on your own or at an inanimate object.

As soon as you express your anger towards another person you damage the relationship and lower your personal dignity and self-esteem. You may feel better at that moment but the damage done to yourself and to others is permanent.

It is a similar situation with what may be regarded as positive emotions such as joy and excitement. Yes, express those emotions but do so within the boundaries of sensibility and responsibility.

We are emotional and it is better to express your emotions rather than to bottle them up inside of you. However, you are in control. This is your life, your intellect, your intuition and your emotions. Express each part of you but control each to the best of your ability.

Week 10

Exercises

1. Listen to music, watch a show, look at photographs, sing, dance, paint, cook, walk or involve yourself with any activity that gives you joy, happiness and satisfaction. From time to time, throughout the activity, pause and soak in the emotion. Let that emotion fill your whole self, body, mind and spirit.

2. Every so often, no matter what you are doing, smile and take 30 seconds to think of something that makes you happy.

3. Think of something that triggers a negative response. The response may be anger, sadness, frustration, worry, guilt or any negative emotion. Say, "I am beyond such negativity." Now sing your favourite song and dance around the room, think of thoughts that fill you with joy and happiness or engage yourself in an activity that you are passionate about.

4. Watch a film or television show or read a newspaper that triggers an emotional response. Begin with something that will trigger a minor emotional response not with something that will cause you immense pain, sorrow, anger or grief.
   Monitor your feelings and see if you can watch or read with total detachment. At the end of the show say, "I am beyond such negativity." Spend a few minutes filling your world with happy and joyful thoughts.

5. Have a friend or your partner play the devil's advocate and say negative things about you to you. After your friend has finished say, "I am beyond such negativity." Remain totally detached. Then, turn the negative statement into a positive statement and smile.

Week 11

Positive Thinking

Along with controlling your emotions comes the next task of controlling your thoughts.

Always think on the positive side.

Negative thoughts create negative self-talk, which, in turn, creates negative actions.

As the saying goes, "water will always find its own level." If you think, talk and act in a negative fashion, you not only attract negative energy and negative people but also attract negative experiences.

Throughout our life we are sent plenty of challenges to deal with. We also experience plenty of situations where there are lessons to be learned. Why would we want to attract more challenges with a constant stream of negativity?

So, always think positive thoughts and appreciate what is good in your life.

This is not a case of being over-optimistic, looking at the world through rose-coloured glasses or having a mind full of wishful thinking.

This is a case of being realistic but in a positive manner.

For example, if you are saving for a holiday. Be realistic. Put away funds that you can afford or cut down on something that will allow you to put funds away. Give yourself a reasonable time frame to save. When you think in a positive fashion it is amazing how many other things fall into place to assist you with your quest.

Positive thoughts create a positive, "can-do" attitude. Simple but true.

Week 11

Exercises

1. First thing in the morning, before you go to bed or during the day when you have a minute or two, think of as many positive things as you can. It does not matter what they are, so long as they are positive.

2. Place items, ones that give you positive thoughts, around your house, at work or wherever you spend a lot of time. When you spy one of these items spend a few seconds contemplating some positive thoughts. Feel the emotion that is attached to these positive thoughts.

3. When you have some free time practice changing negative thoughts into positive thoughts. Sit quietly and reflect on the negative thoughts you have had. Cancel each negative thought and turn it into a positive thought. For example, change, "I can't lose weight." Into "I am losing weight." Here is another example, "There is so much to do. I can't do it all." Change this to, "I am doing what is important and necessary."

4. When a person or situation is frustrating you and challenging you with negative emotions and behaviours do this for the seven days. With your thoughts, send the person or people a bunch of pink balloons filled with love. If the challenge is a place then send a pink cloud full of love to spread throughout the entire area.

5. Be aware of your thought patterns. When you have a negative thought, cancel it out immediately and replace it with a positive thought.

Week 12

Thinking in the Present

Once you begin to think consistently in the positive you can also begin to think in the present.

There is a vast difference between wishful thinking and thinking in the present, even if the present is still in the future.

Does this sound confusing? Possibly, so let us clarify the situation.

Wishful thinking is the continual expression of a desire that will almost never come to fruition. For example, if you keep thinking. "If only, one day or when." This type of expression is in the future and will always stay in the future.

When you use the thought, "I am" it tells a whole different story.

For example, there will be times when you are unhappy or despondent. Once you tell yourself "I am happy" and begin to sing one of your favourite songs it will create a change to the positive.

On the other hand if you say, "I will be happy when." You will be waiting for the "when" to eventually occur and it probably never will occur.

This is a simple example but the application is suitable to all situations.

By thinking in the present and the positive you are bringing that situation into creation. If you keep putting it in the future, it stays in the future.

As usual, be realistic, but always think in the positive and in the present.

Week 12

Exercises

1. Sit quietly or meditate on your personal qualities or the rewarding aspects of your life. Think in the positive. Think in the present. Here are some examples. I am a happy person. I have a welcoming smile. I am kind to animals. I am content with my job. I love my children. I am good company. I like who I am.

2. Sit quietly or meditate on some personal qualities or something that you would like that you have not yet brought into reality. Think of these things or attributes in the positive and in the present. Here are some possible examples. I am always calm in a crisis. I cope very well with my boss's tantrums. I am the perfect weight for my height. I always eat healthy food.

3. Be aware of your thought patterns. When you have a thought that is in the future or the past, cancel it out immediately and replace it with a thought that is expressed in the present. Here is an example. I'll stop gambling when I win the jackpot. Change this to, I never gamble and I am wealthy.

Week 13

Positive Self-talk

Once you begin to get your thinking in the present and in the positive, your next task is to work on your self-talk.

As with your thinking, your task is to talk in the present and in the positive.

Exclude statements like, "when I win the lotto." "I will lose weight and get fit when." These statements are in the future and will most probably stay in the future.

This is not to say never plan for the future. Planning is good. Goal-setting will work if it is realistic. The idea is to bring the future to you and not to push it away and into the realm of always being the future.

Always listen and monitor your self-talk.

You not only have to eliminate the talk that is in the future but also those words that are indecisive.

The word "try' is the best example of indecision.

This is important to understand, you either do something or you don't do something.

If you want to go for a ride on a horse, you either do or you don't. You cannot try to ride a horse. You may not have the best technique but if you are on a horse, you are riding. If you want to lose weight, it is no use saying, "I am trying to lose weight." You are either losing weight or not losing weight.

Your self-talk is so important. Always listen to yourself.

Remember, from this point onwards, you are talking in the present and in the positive.

Week 13

Exercises

1. At least three times a day, say 5 things about yourself that are in the positive and in the present. "I am" or "I have" will begin most of these statements. Here are some examples. "I am content with who I am." I am good at my job." "I am fit and healthy." "I have incredible endurance." "I have an amazing family." "I love my children."

2. Write some of these positive statements and place them in positions where you will notice them. Place them next to or on the mirror, on the back of the toilet door, on the fridge door, on a wall or chest of drawers next to your bed, on the passenger seat of your car, on the front of your mobile phone cover and similar places. When you notice these statements, smile and say them to yourself.

3. At least once a day, deliberately limit your conversation or how much talking you do. This is not to be rude. This exercise allows you time to assess what you say and involve the other people more fully. Ask questions instead of making statements or expressing your opinion.

4. Monitor your self-talk. Listen to what you say. Always make your words positive and in the present.

Week 14

Turning Negative Talk into Positive Talk

It is easy to get into a bad habit. We just do the same thing over and over until we do it without even thinking about what we are doing.

Good habits work in the same way. If we do a positive thing over and over, we eventually continue with that behaviour without even thinking about it.

However, to change from a bad habit to a good habit takes a lot of awareness. However, it can be done.

So, how do we change our negative talk into positive talk?

The first step is to recognize our negative talk, be it self-talk or in conversation with others.

The second step is to cancel out the negative comment and replace it with a positive one. This is done immediately and with no emotion.

For example, if you say, "There are always so many bills to pay. I'll never have any money." Immediately change that to, "There are always bills to pay and I'll always have money left to do what I want to do."

The same rules apply if another person says something about you.

Using a similar example, if a friend says, "You never have any money." Immediately cancel that and say, "I always have money."

Changing negative talk into positive talk is all a matter of awareness. Be on your guard and you will soon find a bad habit is replaced with a good habit and your self-esteem will thank you and respond accordingly.

Week 14

Exercises

1. Write down several negative things that people say about you. They may be true or they may be false, it doesn't really matter. Read the first sentence. Reply by changing the negative statement into a positive statement. For example, you may write: People say that I lack confidence. Read the statement and then say quietly, "I am confident in everything that I do." Continue with the other negative statements that you have written down and change them into positive statements.

2. Work with your partner, a family member or close friend. Spend a few minutes each day on changing negative talk into positive talk. Take it in turns. Your friend should say something negative about you. For example, words like, "You always start something but never finish it." Your reply would be, "I always complete all of my projects." If your friend also adds, "Yes, that is true." This addition will reinforce that positive affirmation. After the first one, swap roles. Complete 4 or 5 examples.

3. Listen to your self-talk and what others say about you. If you or others make a negative comment about you, cancel it out immediately and replace it with a positive statement. Even if your positive statement is not yet true, always state it firmly and with conviction.

Week 15

Positive Action

It is true that "actions speak louder than words." It is also true that "talk is cheap."

Honour is an important quality. When we are true to our word we honour ourselves, the people we deal with and the divine universe.

When we plan or say we are going to do something and commit to those plans and words with action, we are being honourable.

Once you understand that action is a commitment to your word, you gain a better understanding of why each question or request that is presented to you has only a yes or no answer.

Anything but a yes or no answer blurs your course of action. It allows for excuses.

You also gain a better understanding of why it is important to say "no" and not to be coerced into a "yes" response. For when you say "yes" and fail to keep that commitment, you let yourself and others down.

How many New Year's resolutions have fallen by the wayside? After several attempts at change, we find it easier to give up. If your action does not follow your word then it is better to remain silent.

Hopefully, you will also gain a better understanding why words like "try" should be eliminated from your vocabulary.

If you say, "I am trying to give up smoking." What does that mean? There are words but no action. Nothing changes and everything remains the same. Take action and honour your word.

Week 15

Exercises

1. In the morning spend a few minutes writing down a list of 5 tasks that you have the time and the capability of doing before the day is through and you go off to bed. As you complete each task, place a big tick beside them. Keep the tasks simple and realistic.

2. Each day add another task to your list of 5. You may write the same tasks down each day or you may change several or all of them. By the end of the week your list will have 11 daily tasks to complete.

3. Pause and think before you commit to a request. Ask yourself if the task that is asked of you can be done straight away. If the answer is yes and you are content to take on the task then go ahead and agree to the commitment. If the task cannot be done straight away, but you feel you can handle it, and are happy to take it on, then, give a time commitment as to when you can begin. If you say you can begin in an hour, then it is essential to keep to that time frame. If you need to reassess you may do so. However, allow yourself no more than 2 deferrals. After the third strike, this task is out of the question. You politely contact the other party, apologize and say no, this task cannot be done today. By the way, you do not need to forward an excuse or reason.

1. Keep your commitments simple and realistic. Always keep your word. If time, equipment or knowledge does not allow you the ability to say yes, then say no.

Week 16

Dealing with Family

Most of us have to deal with our family. As children we have no choice. As adults, we do have a choice.

Families often present complicated relationships. There is no manual on how to raise a child. There are often loving and nurturing examples of the relationship between parent and child. However, there are also strained and even hostile relationships as well.

The relationship between siblings is also fraught with varying degrees of love, admiration, jealousy, resentment and all manner of emotions.

The key to improving your self-esteem is to understand that not all family relationships are a success.

Each of us is under immense social pressure to get along with all members of our family. We feel the obligation, especially at times of celebration such as Christmas, birthdays, graduations, weddings and anniversaries.

Yet, there are situations when this does not happen. There is conflict and with that conflict is the associated guilt.

Honesty is so important when dealing with family matters and family relationships.

For the sake of your self-esteem, your dignity and your mental well-being there are times when you need to be honest and say to family members that you find dealing with them in certain situations too much of a strain and you will not be attending or adding to the conversation. This you will do with honesty and without guilt.

Week 16

Exercises

1. It is important to understand that you are part of a family. It is also important to understand that you may find certain members of your family a challenge. In fact, you may not like them. If that is the way things are then deal with the relationships with honesty and strength. You may need to sever the relationship. If you need to keep a family relationship then every day say quietly, "I am happy to be part of my family."

2. Each day choose a member of your family and reflect on the things that you have in common or the good times you shared. Never dwell on the negative, always dwell on the positive.

3. Contact a family member. If a phone call is too challenging then begin with a text or email. Keep the message short and simple. You may say something like you were thinking of them, of the good times you shared, wishing them health and happiness and success in what they are doing.

4. With family members or at family gatherings that are a challenge, keep your side of the conversation brief and limited in content. Practice making a statement and then asking a question. For example, you may state that your job is fine. You then ask, "How is your work?" or "Are you still working for the same company or have you changed your situation?"

5. When conversations are a challenge, never argue about or justify your situation. In challenging conversations you play politics. You state your position or opinion once, maybe twice, and then ask a question or change the topic of conversation.

Week 17

Choosing your Friends

You generally are in no position to choose your family but you are always in a position to choose your friends.

Friendship is important. Generally we all need the special and supportive relationship of good friends. We need people in our lives to share our experiences, to discuss important or trivial issues and to be there for us in times of fun, success, crisis or hardship. After all we are social beings.

The key consideration with friends revolves around two issues, being positive and being accepted for who you are.

It is always going to be difficult to be in the present and the positive if the friends you associate with are continually being negative or desire to live in the past, the future or a world of social fantasy.

Negative friends engage in negative talk and negative actions. If you find that your friends continually gossip, spread rumours or put down other acquaintances, wouldn't you think they do the same thing to you.

When you are positive it is so much easier to find like-minded, positive friends.

The other issue with friendship is that many friendships are built on similar interests and stability. Be aware of friends who are prepared to hold you back when you begin to make changes. This is conditional friendship. There is no need to worry because as you change you will discard these old friends and find new, more supportive friends.

Week 17

Exercises

1. Make a list of your friends. Write down one word or phrase that describes your relationship. This is not to be seen as a popularity contest of your friends or for your friends. We are attracted to our friends for all kinds of reasons and archetypal combinations. The idea behind this exercise is to recognize a positive relationship and a negative relationship. If you recognize a negative relationship you may wish to enact a change in the relationship. That choice is up to you.

2. Similar to the exercise involving your family members, each day choose a friend and reflect on the things that you have in common or the good times you shared. Never dwell on the negative, always dwell on the positive.

3. Ditto with contacting a friend. If your time is limited you may not wish to use the phone and so a text, email or message may be more suitable. Again, keep the message short and simple, and once again, you may say something like you were thinking of them, of the good times you shared, wishing them health and happiness and success in what they are doing. You may wish to add something a little more personal and emotional.

4. Be aware that everything changes. Review your friendships. There are times when you undertake personal changes. The same may be the case with your friends. If a relationship drifts apart, then let it go. Change begets change. A drift in one relationship always creates a vacuum that is soon filled by the forming of another relationship.

Week 18

Friendly Conversations

There are two golden rules that relate to the topic of friendly conversations.

The first rule says never gossip or become involved in personality clashes. We have entered the age of gossip, rumour, innuendo, personal opinion, scandal, put downs and bullying. Newspapers, magazines and social media are full of all these damaging aspects.

Stay away from such trivia and avoid the nonsense.

This is not to say that you need to avoid the media. You can if you feel that the negativity affects you. That is the right thing for you. However, if you consider it important to be informed and up-to-date with what is happening in the world then that is also right for you. The key is to remain objective and control your emotional reactions.

This is even more important within your social group. You have no right to impinge on another's reputation through gossip, rumour, innuendo, put-downs and the like. "If you can't say anything nice, then don't say anything at all," is a motto to put into practice.

The second rule says that conversations between people are private.

If two people are talking about you, then it is none of your business.

Never react to what has been said or what has reportedly been said about you. Once again, it is none of your business.

However, if gossip enters the public domain and is damaging to your reputation then you have the right to take action. Otherwise stay pure and stay away from personality conflicts.

Week 18

Exercises

1. Make a list of 7 friends or family members. Write a list of positive words or phrases that best describe them. Whenever one of these people comes to mind take a moment to reflect on them and how you best describe them.

2. Acquire a copy of one of Australia's magazines like 'Women's Weekly', 'New Idea', 'Woman's Day', 'That's Life', 'TV Week' or whichever one you fancy. Choose one of the articles and read it carefully. Distinguish what is fact and what is gossip or rumour. Reflect on your own conversations and determine if you converse with facts or with gossip and rumours.

3. Be aware of the conversations that you participate in. If the conversation involves gossip and rumour announce it as such or choose not to join in with such speculation. Always respect other people's privacy and their decisions.

4. Be willing to defend another with the truth if you are privy to the truth. This is not permission to begin or continue an argument with a third party. However, this is permission to state the truth in an honest and objective way.

5. If a person relates a story or conversation about what a third party has said about you, pause and consider your response. If you consider the matter trivial, ignore or dismiss what you have been told and change the topic of conversation. Never denigrate the third party. If you consider it a serious matter, terminate that conversation and seek out the third party to establish the truth. You can then decide on the appropriate course of action.

Week 19

Friendly Actions

 As a follow on from friendly conversations, many of the same criteria apply to friendly actions.

What you say and how you behave, defines your personality, morals and ethics.

If you could be objective, stand back from who you are and truthfully judge your words and your actions, what would you see?

Do you like how you behave? Are you friendly and courteous? Do you listen to what others have to say? Do you dominate the conversation with your concerns, worries or opinions? Are you willing to help others in their time of need? Are you responsible? How you treat the environment that surrounds you? Do you show respect to others and treat them as individuals?

"Do unto others as you would have them do unto you," is a fine saying.

Be aware that this approach does not mean that you have to agree to every demand or request. Also, it does not mean you allow people to walk over you.

Always maintain your strength and your personal power. However, always call upon your strength and personal power to act righteously.

Be true to who you are but also be a contributor to the betterment of your family, social circle, neighbourhood and society.

Be discerning and always be aware of your actions.

Week 19

Exercises

1. Always remember to smile. When you meet acquaintances or strangers greet them with a smile. When you see someone doing something positive, acknowledge their actions with a smile of approval. If you cross paths on a regular basis with a total stranger greet them with a smile. A smile costs you nothing but it can certainly brighten up another person's day.

2. Greet your friends and family with a hug. Make your hug warm and sincere.

3. You can follow up your hug with a compliment. Make the compliment positive and sincere. "You look fantastic in that outfit." "Your hair looks wonderful." "I love the way you are always on time." "You look ready for action." These are just a few examples.

4. If a hug and a compliment seems uncomfortable for some friends or acquaintances then begin with a question. "Have you had a good day today?" "Have you parked the car close by?" "Where did you get that cool outfit?" These are only examples. Like everything else your compliments or questions need to be sincere and relevant. If you are unable to think of suitable words, then, at the very least, smile.

5. This week, purchase and give a small gift to someone you care about.

6. This week, offer to help someone you care about complete a small task. Devote an hour of your time to a family member, friend, neighbour or charity. Take someone for a meal or to a film. It doesn't have to be time consuming or expensive, after all, it is the thought and action that counts.

Week 20

Know Who You Are

Awareness of what you say and how you act begins with knowing who you are.

To give you an extreme example, the negative addict will never heal or change their behaviour unless they admit to who they are and recognize their negative behaviour.

This is the same for all of us.

Until we have an understanding of who we are, we will often stay in the dark or in denial as to our actions and our behaviour.

Change comes with knowledge, understanding and a desire to do things differently.

Self-assessment is a good tool.

Through my archetype workshops, I am in the fortunate position to assist people discover their personal archetypes. We find out exactly who they are and why they do what they do. Archetypes are valuable tools in self-discovery and self-empowerment.

There are other tools and other methods that allow for self-discovery and self-empowerment. It is up to you to decide which is suited to your needs and which allows you the comfort of self-discovery.

The important thing is to take your courage, some time and discover your true self. This is not always an easy task for you have to be brutally honest and have complete trust in the facilitator or consultant.

However, it is a task well worth undertaking, so this week, take up the challenge and go on a voyage of self-discovery.

Week 20

Exercises

1. Book yourself into or take a course into self-discovery. I find that archetypes are brilliant at unveiling who you are and why you do the things you do. There are other methods but find a facilitator or a course that appeals to and suits you.

2. Make a list of words and phrases that best describe you. Divide the list into positive and negative characteristics or personality traits.

3. Write down the occasions or situations when you use your positive characteristics or personality traits.

4. Write down the occasions or situations when you use your negative characteristics or personality traits. Examine your negative words and phrases and write down a positive word or phrase that has the opposite meaning to the negative word or phrase.

5. From this time onwards, focus on and use the positive words. Turn these positive words into positive actions.

6. Examine each occasion and situation and find a positive aspect. Look at how you can expand this positive aspect.

Week 21

Understand Who You Are

When you know who you are you can begin to understand why you act the way you do and why you behave in the way you do.

As an example, let us return to the discussion surrounding archetypes. If you know you have a Queen archetype, you will understand that you take charge especially in the area that you consider your realm. This is natural behaviour for a person with a Queen archetype.

Unfortunately, you may have to share your duties with another Queen and this may lead to a conflict involving duties and territory. Alternatively, you may be subject to a boss or organizational hierarchy who frustrate you with the incompetence of a Fool archetype, focus on trivialities fit for a Princess, rule with the deceit of a Thief or the cruelty of a Bully. In all of these cases your self-esteem is not only challenged but also open to direct hits of unworthiness and of being consistently undervalued.

When we know and understand who we are, we also become aware of our negative behaviour traits and our positive behaviour traits. Understanding gives us a choice. We can choose to stay the way we are or we can choose to change. We can choose to play to our strengths and positive characteristics or we can choose to dwell in our weaknesses and negative characteristics.

Finally, always consider your emotions. Understanding our emotions undoubtedly affects our self-esteem. The more we involve ourselves in situations that give joy, satisfaction, identity, belonging, contentment and the like, the more balanced we are and greater care is taken of our self-esteem.

Week 21

Exercises

1. Make a list of the people you care about. Write down a word or phrase that best describes your relationship or how you treat these people. Change any negative words or phrases to the opposite positive words and phrases. Spend a few moments thinking of how you can relate to that person with a positive pattern of behaviour.

2. Repeat the same exercise with people that you have to work with but with whom you may not share a thoroughly enjoyable relationship.

3. Make a list of the times, places, events or people that cause you frustration, anger, resentment, jealousy, depression or any other negative emotions. If possible, avoid these situations. If that is not possible, spend some time identifying the cause of these negative emotions. When you have identified the cause, write down an affirmation that expresses the opposite of what you feel and how you can cope with the situation. For example, if your boss causes you frustration because you know of more efficient ways to do business, yet your advice is ignored. Affirm, "I am at ease with my boss and my job because my ideas are brilliant and are ready to be accepted."

4. Spend time in, at least, one activity each day that gives you enjoyment, pleasure, satisfaction, joy or a sense of achievement. When you have finished that activity, pause and soak up the emotion. Affirm, "This is how I feel every moment of every day."

Week 22

Changing Your Attitude

Always remember that more than anything else, self-esteem is an attitude. This attitude affects us in four ways.

Firstly, our attitude determines our behaviour or how we act in all situations. For example, if we do not wish to be in a certain place or be involved in a certain activity we often act withdrawn and lacking enthusiasm. Alternatively, if we want to be there or be involved we are often keen and energetic.

Secondly, our attitude determines our emotions and how we express those emotions. As with the first example, we may be grumpy in a situation we would rather avoid or we may be excited in a task we are keen to be involved in.

Thirdly, our attitude influences our risk-taking. Do we involve ourselves one hundred percent? Do we throw ourselves into a challenge no matter the personal risk to our physical, emotional or psychological well-being? Do we care or take notice of what others may say about us?

Fourthly, our attitude suggests which of our abilities we use and to the extent we use them. If we are keen to participate in a given situation, we will use all of our talents and abilities to achieve our goal or the group goal. We are also more likely to be switched on as to which personal traits and talents are needed for that circumstance.

So take note. If something or someone is a challenge, the first thing to do is to change your attitude. Begin with small items. Then, as your confidence grows, your attitude and that increased confidence will allow you to take on larger, more complex situations and challenges.

Week 22

Exercises

1. Always begin with a small task. Choose an activity that you consider menial or frustrating. As you involve yourself with tackling this task, think of all the positives that come from this activity. The task may be something as simple as making the bed. Focus on the fact that you have a bed to make. Focus on your physical abilities that enable you to undertake this activity. Focus on how comforting it will be that evening, when you are tired and ready for a rest, to be able to climb into a welcoming, beautifully made bed. Focus on how neat, tidy or elegant your bed is when it is made and looking at its best. Place a small decoration as a finishing touch. Stand back and admire your work and congratulate yourself on a job well done.

2. The following day choose a more complicated task. Go up in small degrees of difficulty and do not over-reach. Involve yourself in the same process.

3. Use your list from the third exercise on the previous topic. Take one situation or person at a time. Identify the aspect that is causing you to have a negative attitude. Affirm a positive attitude. Let us use a wayward teenager as an example. Affirm that this is their life and their responsibility. Let go of or ignore the minor disagreements. Make the teenager aware of the consequences for major discretions. Be prepared to pick up the pieces on some occasions but not for all of them.

4. Work on your fears and your risk-taking. Concentrate on a small fear. Take on an activity that is minor in nature but one that confronts this fear. Progress, step by step, and always acknowledge your achievement.

Week 23

Taking Things Personally

There are many things that happen to us and many things said to us or about us that we take personally.

If something negative happens, we often blame ourselves. This causes guilt which damages our self-esteem. Many people, of course, blame others. This is an attempt to protect their self-esteem while damaging another's self-esteem.

Taking the blame and taking responsibility are two different things. Blame is always associated with finding fault, attributing guilt and wanting reparation, even revenge. Responsibility is accepting that we could have done better and that we have learned from this experience. It is part of the human experience to make mistakes or errors of judgment. However, mistakes made in good faith are very different from deliberate actions. Check your intention. If your intention is good and honourable and things go astray, then take responsibility but never take the blame, the guilt and the personal hit to your self-esteem.

Remember too, what people say to each other is none of your business. If you have heard that something negative was said about you then, eliminate the negative and change it to the positive.

What is said to you by another and what you say to them is your business. If what is said to you is negative, consider it briefly. If you know it to be untrue, correct the statement to the other person and change it to the positive.

The rule is; if what is said to you and about you is a compliment then, and only then, take it personally, with both joy and humility.

Week 23

Exercises

1. Every day this week meditate or visualize. This only needs to be a short meditation or visualization. Picture a film of white light surrounding your entire body. This film has tiny pores that allow all the compliments and positive emotions to enter your mind and your heart. However, all negative words, actions and energies are blocked, unable to penetrate the light and so they bounce back into the ether.

2. In moments of unawareness, stress or pressure when a negative comment or action does enter your psyche, visualize your protective white light consuming that negative energy. Reinforce the process with a positive statement.

3. When encountering moments of indecision ask this question, "Will this dilemma be important in 12 months' time?" If the answer is no, then let the matter rest. If the answer is yes, then take action.

4. Consider an occasion when you took a comment, an action or a failure personally. Consider the importance and realism of the matter. Is that matter still important to you now? If not send in your protective white light to consume this event and the consequential emotions. If it is important to you now, then examine ways to change the situation. Examine how realistic the matter was. Was it a promise or a commitment that you made at the time that, with hindsight, was unrealistic and could never be kept. If you hold onto any guilt, regret or shame allow your protective white light to devour these feelings. Follow this examination of the events with a positive affirmation or statement.

Week 24

Finding Your Passion

One of the most effective ways of preserving and improving your self-esteem is to find and pursue your passion.

As you are an individual, your passion may be in any number of areas. Your passion may be in the creative field. It may be in exploration and pioneering. It may be in travel and adventure. It may be in dealing with and protecting plants or animals. It may be in the field of human interest and support. It may be in making money, in business or entrepreneurial ventures. It may be in collecting and restoring ancient or unique artefacts. It may be in teaching and working with children. The choices are many and each choice is yours.

There are plenty of mundane issues and procedures in life that we are obliged to fulfil. Always do these with grace and contentment. Never get hassled by the small things in life. Do the dishes with enjoyment. Play with the children with enthusiasm. Go to work with commitment and purpose. If you are passionate about any of these issues then you stand in your power.

If you find there are things in your life that are a frustration and a challenge, there are two things you can do. Firstly, change your attitude. Secondly, find an activity that stimulates you and sets you free from the mundane and the repetitive.

Whatever you do, spend and invest some time on you.

This has nothing to do with being selfish. It has everything to do with your physical, emotional and psychological well-being.

Find your passion and pursue it with vigour and intent.

Week 24

Exercises

1. Spend 5 to 10 minutes in a brainstorming activity. With pen and paper write down all the things you like doing, all the things you are good at and all the things you would like to do. Highlight 5 of those activities. Are these activities in your life? If not, take steps to include at least one of these activities. If they are all in your life, take steps to be more involved in at least one of those activities.

2. Consider how you spend your time. If you are a visual or a highly organized person you may wish to put your daily or weekly schedule onto paper. How much time are you devoting to the activities that you are passionate about? How much time are you devoting to other matters, either essential or non-essential? Are you able to eliminate non-essential activities and give more time to what you truly enjoy?

3. Attitude is important. There are aspects and activities in life that we feel an obligation to. Consider your attitude to each of these activities. Let us use work as an example. If you love your job and are passionate about what you do, that is fantastic. There are no challenges in this area of your life. If you find work a challenge but have little alternative as to your situation, then examine your attitude. Work is a means of making money. Money pays your bills and gives you the means of participating in activities that you enjoy. View work as a means of supporting your passion and achievements. Your attitude then focuses on the positive rather than the negative.

Week 25

Changes

Nothing stays the same. Everything changes, including you.

The key is for you to activate the changes within you and the changes within your life. Please understand that you do not and cannot control every aspect of your life. However, there are many aspects that you can control.

The first and most important aspect you can control is your attitude. You choose your attitude, nobody else does. If something is frustrating you, then change your attitude towards the task, person or situation. You may, if possible, need to cut that task, person or situation out of your life.

The second aspect you can control is your emotions. Again if some task, person or situation contributes to a negative and uncontrolled emotion then the same two things apply. Make a change in your life and cut out whatever is the source of anger, frustration, sorrow, envy, disappointment, depression and the like. If you are unable to disassociate yourself from the task, person or situation then change your attitude and aim any of your negative emotions at an inanimate object.

Remember that change should always be for the better.

Look at changing negative habits or patterns of behaviour into positive habits or patterns of behaviour. Look at changing your negative thoughts and words into positive thoughts and words. Finally, cut out the negative people in your life and replace them with positive, supporting people. We are very much influenced by the company we keep.

Week 25

Exercises

1. Every day this week change at least one aspect of your daily life. Take the train to work rather than drive the car. Eat a healthy meal rather than getting take-away. Take a walk after dinner instead of watching television. Prepare a small patch of garden or purchase a large tub and plant some vegetable seedlings. Spend your time on the computer writing a story or your biography rather than playing games or looking at social media.

2. This week take up the challenge of beginning a new activity. Choose something that is rewarding but not too great a challenge. Up until now, what have you excused you from that stimulates you? Here are some possibilities. You could join a book club, a choir or an amateur theatre group. How about gathering a few friends and facilitating a workshop or circle of interest. The possibilities are endless. Take a small risk, make a positive change and take action.

3. If there is change in your life, embrace that change. Even if the change presents challenges, look for the positives and the lessons that are learned.

4. If you have made a decision that later does not suit your needs then make another decision to change your situation. There is no need to take on regret or guilt if something does not work out. Decide on another course of action and take steps in a new direction.

Week 26

Priorities

Many of us lead very busy lives and the expectation to be involved in so many things can, at times, be overwhelming. At times we can get lost in all the demands of relationships, family, home, work and friends. We can lose sight of who we are and what is important in our life.

One way to keep ourselves on track is to establish a list of priorities. There are some people who are very good at keeping a "to do" list and ticking off each achievement. This works well in many cases. If you have established this habit, well done, and keep up the good work.

However, not all of us are that organized. Many of us fall into the habit of going off on tangents. Some of us lack the capacity to say, "No" and become involved in situations that waste our time and are of little interest to us. Here is the simple version. Write down a list of three or four areas in your life that are a priority to you for the next eight months. They may include family, health, fitness, education, holiday, work, business, house and garden, new car, more money, a creative project, a new relationship and anything else that you deem important.

Once you have established your list, determine to spend your time and energy on what is on your priority list. Of course, you still need to do the everyday essentials, such as prepare meals. However, when faced with a decision to invest your time and energy, the question is, "is it on my priority list?" If the answer is "Yes" then get involved. If the answer is "No" then abstain. The key is that there is to be no discussion, no argument and no justification.

Week 26

Exercises

1. Establish your priorities list for the next eight months. Stick to the rules:

    (a) Choose 3 or 4 areas of your life. Choose what is especially important to you now and in the foreseeable future.

    (b) Write these areas down on paper or card and display them prominently.

    (c) Apart from what is necessary to run your life, every other activity is examined with relevance to your priority list.

    (d) If an activity fits into your priorities then the answer is yes, you participate. If an activity does not fit into your priorities then the answer is no, no participation.

    (e) The answer is either a yes or a no. There is no room or excuses for maybe.

    (f) Tell the people close to you that this is what you are doing. They may be disappointed when you fail to participate in activities that you normally share.

    (g) There is to be no discussion, no argument and no justification. The answer is either yes or no. You have made a decision and there is no need to justify your decisions to anyone else. Stay strong in your own power.

Week 27

Strengths

One of the best ways to maintain and enhance our self-esteem is to focus on our strengths.

We all have talents and abilities. The key is to develop and improve those talents and abilities. The other important issue is to reward yourself when you have successfully used those talents and abilities. The reward may be as simple as saying, "I did that really well" and follow up with a pat on the back. Alternatively, it may be a monetary reward or a bit of rest and relaxation. Always be aware. Notice when you have done something well and give yourself praise.

Whatever field you are talented in, then use that talent to the best of your ability. Always remember that your ability will improve with practice. Often the most difficult decision is to make a start. Also, remember to move at your own pace.

Finally, never let anyone else distract you from using or displaying your talents and abilities. This is a common situation for teenagers, especially girls. In such circumstances the peer group pressure determines what is acceptable and what is not. Remember, your first requirement is to please yourself and no one else. Take pride in what you do and what you achieve. There is nothing wrong with being proud. It is only when the ego and boasting comes into play that negative attitudes and behaviours come to the fore.

When we have the awareness to focus on our strengths, we begin to achieve. Step by step, accomplishment by accomplishment, we become experienced. Once we have established a level of achievement and experience we are both capable and confident to expand our level and range of expertise. Your self-esteem will not look back.

Week 27

Exercises

1. Make a list of 7 talents, abilities or qualities that you have. They may be your talent for business, leadership, sporting abilities, teaching, expressing your creative pursuits, caring for others, being positive - examine everything about you. Focus on one of these attributes each day this week. When you find success using that particular strength, give yourself praise and recognition.

2. As you focus on a particular talent each day consider ways in which you could utilize that talent in a different area of your life. For example, if you are a teacher, consider new pathways or new opportunities where your personal teaching skills could become a vital ingredient for success. Are you passionate about a new project, challenge or something you have wanted to do that could utilize your personal skills?

3. Every day affirm each one of these skills. For example, you may affirm with, "I am brilliant at managing money." "In a crisis I love to take charge." "Painting not only gives me pleasure and satisfaction but an opportunity to express my creative self." "I am an exceptional conversationalist."

Week 28

Physical Strength

If you possess athletic ability, physical strength and prowess then use these natural attributes to your advantage.

Remember to work with your strengths. If you possess physical ability then find activities that use your talent. These abilities may be used to establish a career or for recreation.

Those who possess physical strength and athletic ability have a variety of career options. It is not just the elite sportsperson who depend on their physical prowess. There are a variety of possibilities within the fitness industry, landscaping, home maintenance, transport and the numerous trades. Strength, stamina and endurance are required to succeed in these areas. An indoor position may not be suited to your ability and your needs. If you have physical ability, use it to your advantage.

The other great benefit of physical strength and prowess is that it enables a person to participate and often excel in chosen sporting fields. There are huge benefits for an individual's self-esteem when that individual participates in sport. Fitness, developing ability and talent, concentration and mental awareness, taking a risk, acceptance of winning and losing, working as a team and friendship are all lessons learned from participation in sport. There is also the extra benefit of involvement in a healthy and beneficial form of rest and relaxation.

It is understood that each sporting success maintains and enhances self-esteem. However, it is to be remembered, that in both winning and losing, there exist lessons and experiences beneficial to personal growth and development.

Week 28

Exercises

1. Every day this week engage in an activity that will strengthen your physical self. This activity may be passive or strenuous, depending upon your level of health, fitness and capability. Stay within the boundaries of your capabilities. If you have a health problem always consult a doctor or a medical professional.

   You can do something as simple as taking a walk, going for a swim, bouncing on a trampoline or trying some basic yoga. If exercise isn't something that is within your capabilities or is likely to create stress, then look towards your eating habits. Eat nothing but salads or raw vegetables for the day. You may try fasting for a day. Eliminate sugar for the day. If you are into physical activity or sport then try something different that will strengthen a different part of your physical body.

2. For the purpose of this exercise, physical strength is not just about how many push ups you can do or what weight you can press. Physical strength is also about endurance and mental determination. Go to a project that is only half completed and spend some time during the week finishing this project. It may be an area in the garden, a redecoration of a room, an art work that needs completion, re-organizing your finances or any task that is unfinished. Call upon your endurance and attitude to see this project to a completion. Put your excuses away and take action. When you have finished give yourself praise.

Week 29

Intellectual Ability

When we were of school age there were three important ways that we could succeed. The first, and perhaps the most important, is through our intellect. Academic success plays a vital role in maintaining and enhancing our self-esteem. This was certainly true when we were at school and our intellect also plays an important role now that we are adults.

The other two ways are through our sporting and physical ability and our creativity.

In regard to your intellect, always look for opportunities to use your intellect in a positive way and never in a negative way. Never be distracted and become the perpetrator of cynicism, verbal abuse, put-downs, superiority, intellectual snobbery and the like.

Always use your intellect for the advancement of you, your friends, and your peers and for humanity as a whole. If you have the passion and the capability to improve your qualifications, do so. If you have the passion for learning, then follow your interests and be involved with the subject matter and the learning process. Your self-esteem will be rewarded with both your participation and your success.

Always remember that intellectual ability is not common sense. Both are important attributes that become more effective when practiced together.

The key is always to transfer your intellectual ability and success from thought and study into action. Be a doer as well as a thinker. Look for ways to improve the world around you. The intellect is a wonderful human attribute. Take advantage of your ability.

Week 29

Exercises

1. Take on an activity that will challenge and broaden your intellectual capability. As with every exercise, keep the challenge simple and realistic. Complete a crossword puzzle, write a short story, put the calculator away and complete your accounts or budget with pen, paper and old-fashioned mathematics, join a book club, choose a current topic of conversation and write down the arguments that differ from your opinion, watch a movie and critique it or just stimulate your intellect with something you are passionate about.

2. If there is something in your neighbourhood, in the place where you live, in your country or in the world, that you are passionate about and would like to see changed and improved, then take the time to write a letter to the person in charge or the authority with the power to make change. The authority may be your local council, the Mayor, a politician, a government department, a charity or a business. By all means write about your concerns but also offer a solution or an alternate. Be positive and propose a solution. Expect a personal reply but do not be disappointed with the response. The purpose of the exercise is to clarify your thoughts and make those in authority aware of your concern and an alternative situation.

3. Consider and enrol in further studies, a short workshop or a focus group. Follow your passion. Keep within your means and your time capabilities.

Week 30

Personal Talents

We are all individuals who possess personal talents and attributes. Our talents will not only be in our intellectual and physical abilities but also in our creative and intuitive abilities.

Our ability to act, sing, dance, draw, paint, play a musical instrument and succeed at any number of creative pursuits is so important to us at a personal level. It is also important in that it creates a mechanism to involve others in the creative process and spread the enjoyment of that process.

If you have a creative ability, utilize that ability. Never be concerned with the opinions of others or your personal assessment that compares you with others. "Beauty is in the eye of the beholder" is a truism that should apply to any of your personal creative pursuits.

It is amazing how relaxing and psychologically beneficial participation in the creative process can be. Your self-esteem will be enhanced when you approach your creativity with passion and enjoyment.

Those of us with intuitive abilities have a unique opportunity to teach others, enhance their understanding and provide a source of information and guidance that can add fulfilment and meaning to this world and our place in it. Never underestimate your intuition and how it can be used for your benefit and the benefit of others.

Of equal value are your personal attributes and behaviours. It is amazing how beneficial a smile, a hug, a compliment, a word of encouragement or the willingness to just "be there" can be. Never dismiss or take for granted the influence of one small act of kindness.

Week 30

Exercises

1. Allow yourself 30 minutes every day this week to pursue and improve your personal skills and talents. You may wish to combine the time frame into what suits you and your schedule. For example, you may take 1 hour every second day. Consider what you do creatively. You may wish to reunite with an activity that was once a joy but has been placed in retirement due to changing circumstances and new responsibilities.

2. Listen to your inner child. We all have a Child archetype. Listen to that voice that tells you about the fun things that you did as a child or that you were never allowed to do. For example, your inner child may wish to walk barefoot through a stream, ride a horse, finger paint, dance naked around the house, ride a bike or sleep under the stars. Allow yourself the time and the opportunity to follow at least one fun request.

3. Exercise your intuitive self. Spend a part of the day following your gut feeling. Put your intellect and your emotions aside. Just go with the flow and do whatever seems right at the time. Remember there is to be no thinking. Intuition is an automatic reaction that tells you; this is the right thing to do and this is right for me.

4. Practice being friendly and positive. Smile at strangers, greet acquaintances, hug friends and family, pay compliments, offer to help and be a good listener. Be proud of who you are and how you relate to others. Respect not just the people you like but also the people who challenge you.

Week 31

Skills

Never neglect your skills. Always treat them with respect and use them efficiently and generously. Using your skills is a great way to maintain and enhance your self-esteem.

It does not matter what type of skill you possess. What does matter is how you use those skills.

It may be your ability to make a beautiful object. It may be your ability to invent something that is useful. It may be your ability to make the peace. You may have a talent for solving problems. Whatever your skills are, use them with purpose.

Generally, the more we practice, the better we become. As your skills improve, so does your confidence and your self-esteem. You begin to understand that in certain aspects of your life you have the skills, not just to manage in these circumstances, but to improve the broader situation. This leads to confidence and creates a "can do" attitude. This is about building and enhancing self-esteem.

Humans are adaptable creatures. Many of the skills we learn and develop can be used in different situations. Once we build confidence in one situation we can transfer that skill and confidence to a different situation.

Our self-esteem is our friend. Once we have developed an attitude that reinforces our confidence and have an understanding of our abilities we can make a positive contribution in many of the aspects of life.

Use your skills for personal enhancement, to be a positive influence and role-model for others and to contribute to humanity.

Week 31

Exercises

1. Identify two skills that you have and write them in a positive affirmation. For example, you may write; I am a nurturing and caring mother who raises my children with love and respect. Here is another example. I am incredibly good at solving problems. These are the skills you are going to work on this week.

2. Choose the first of your skills and come up with new ways or new situations that will benefit from the application of your skill. In other words, transfer your skills from the home to work, from work to your leisure activities, from your leisure activities to your family, from your family to your friends. Become adaptive. Be creative. Be innovative.

3. Choose the second of your skills and consider how that skill can be enhanced. Begin a course. Attend a workshop. Seek advice from a mentor. Read a book. Scan the internet. Once you have the information that you need, begin a series of exercises that improve your skill level.

Week 32

Challenges

Life is full of challenges. Some challenges are small in nature while others really test our mettle. Some people appear to lead a charmed life and experience very few challenges, while others seem to face a constant stream of challenges.

Accept your challenges. This is not the same as attracting difficulties through negative behaviours. If we participate in negative activities we should expect negative consequences. Even though you may lead a life with positive attitudes and behaviours, life will still throw challenges in your direction. Accept them and deal with them.

Understand the lessons that come with each challenge. Learn from the experience. Be optimistic. Look for the good or the new direction that may come from a difficult or challenging experience.

Be realistic with each challenge. Never let the little things in life cause you anxiety, stress or guilt. These emotions damage our self-esteem. If you are caught in traffic that is the way things are. The lesson may be to teach you patience. Use that time to relax or plan. Your attitude will determine how you react to each situation. Let the small challenges pass. If what is occurring now is not important in twelve months' time then it is not important now.

If you are faced with a difficult or intense challenge, manage to keep things in perspective. If you have a serious health issue, if there is a death in your family or with someone close to you, if you lose your job, always remember to focus on the challenge. Never stress or worry about what might or might not happen. Take one step at a time. Decide on a course of action, take small steps and build on each achievement.

Week 32

Exercises

1. Each day choose a person, a situation or an event that challenges you. Begin with a small challenge and progress to the larger, more complex challenges.

2. Take the first challenge and look for the positives that surround that challenge. For example, if the boss is demanding and prone to tantrums, consider the good aspects for working in that business or organization. Do not take this as an acceptance of bullying or being taken advantage of. You still need to stand in your strength and take official action in regards to your rights in the workplace. However, if it is a personality clash or a difference of opinion over work processes then take up the challenge.

    Look at the positives. If the pay is reasonable, then that is a positive. If travel to and from your workplace is quick or enjoyable, then that is a positive. If you have time away from work for family and leisure, then that is a positive. If you enjoy the company of others who work there, then that is a positive. If you get satisfaction from your responsibilities, then that is a positive.

3. Be proactive rather than reactive. Let us use the work scenario once more. If you can see some difficulty approaching, then go to the boss and mention the possibility. Always make this exchange cordial, short and precise. Make your statement with no argument or justification and then excuse yourself. If the problem occurs, do not accept blame or responsibility. You simply remind the boss of your previous conversation. Once again, never argue or justify.

Week 33

Physical Challenges

There will be times when we are physically challenged. Accidents occur. From time to time, sickness and illness catch up with us. As we become older we may not be able to do the things we once did and took for granted. We may need to change our lifestyle.

As with all challenges we need to keep things in perspective.

If the challenge is small in nature then understand that life will go on and a return to normality is only a matter of time. If you are ill, you will recover. If you have broken a bone, it will heal. If you have an accident, then seek treatment and undertake a period of rest and recovery. If there are matters that need dealing with that are now beyond your capabilities, then seek the help of your partner, a family member, a friend or an agency.

Serious physical challenges require a different approach. Often, an intense physical challenge demands a change in our daily thought pattern, our attitude and our behaviour. A serious illness, accident or event rearranges our priorities.

In such cases the focus needs to be on ourselves. The emphasis changes to lifestyle, treatments and procedures. The task is to focus on recovery or adjustment.

With serious physical challenges we need to deal with one issue at a time. Yes, we understand that there may be a multitude of things to consider. However, it is important not to let the situation overwhelm you. Decide on a flexible plan then take one step at a time. Call upon the strong aspects of your self-esteem to manage each event.

Week 33

Exercises

1. Each day examine what you are capable of doing. Be realistic. If you achieve more than you planned, then that is a positive. Give yourself credit for what you have achieved. If you fail to achieve what you have planned, remain positive. Cancel any feeling of guilt or failure with a positive affirmation. "Circumstances were a challenge and I still managed to make great progress." Then, reassess your task and give yourself credit for your endurance and your adaptability.

2. Every day affirm your personal good health. You may be in the middle of a health crisis, yet still affirm your good health. Say something like, "I am fit. I am healthy. I am full of life and vitality."

3. Centre your attention and your focus on you. This is not being selfish. This is being practical. If you have physical or health challenges it is imperative that you are the focus. You cannot assist and be of service to others if you are not physically well or capable of rendering assistance. Look after yourself.

4. If you are going through a health crisis, set your focus on a positive outcome. Find an illustration or a photograph that represents your journey. It may be something like the yellow brick road. It may be a tunnel with white or golden light at the tunnel's end. It may be a bridge or a long road across a wide valley or large river. Give yourself praise every day for taking another step on your journey.

Week 34

Psychological Challenges

Everything that happens to us influences our self-esteem. The thing to remember is that our self-esteem is an attitude. Therefore, our self-esteem and our attitude to each particular circumstance determine our reaction to everything that happens to us.

Severe psychological challenges are the events that can really test our attitude and our self-esteem. The difficulty with psychological challenges is that many of them happen to us when we are young, either as children or teenagers. At these ages we have limited control of the situation and limited life experiences and knowledge in how to deal with these challenges. It is not until we reach adulthood that we can reassess the experience and seek an understanding, treatment or healing. By this stage our self-esteem has been damaged.

Abuse can take many forms. The damage that is done is a case-by-case scenario. It depends entirely on the events, the duration, the individuals involved, the relationships and the initial level of self-esteem of the victim. The good news is that our self-esteem can be repaired. Bit by bit we can change our attitude and strengthen our self-esteem.

The first thing needed is an understanding that the abuse has ceased. This is not always the case. A child, psychologically abused by their father, may form relationships with an abusive partner. Familiarity has strong motivation. Understand yourself and ensure that you are not in a similar type of abusive situation. The second thing needed is the realization is that you are now an adult and you are now in control. You control your attitude. You can seek treatment and healing. You, and only you, can strengthen your self-esteem.

Week 34

Exercises

1. If you have suffered psychological trauma, this is the week for action. If you need to consult a professional, then do so. If you need to share a traumatic experience, consult a close and discerning friend. If you have a secret of mistreatment of any kind, this is the week to share that secret. You will always carry those memories but now is the time to release that negative energy.

2. Once the trauma is shared and acknowledged you can begin the healing process. Exorcize any guilt or responsibility. Turn negative thoughts and words into positive thoughts and words. When thoughts like, "I am to blame" or "It was my fault" come to the fore, change them. Say, "I am innocent of any wrongdoing."

3. Examine all of your relationships. Which relationships are positive and which relationships are negative? Do any of your relationships continue a pattern of psychological mistreatment? If so, take steps to terminate this relationship. If that is not possible, look for ways to stand in your power and change the relationship. This is exactly what you are doing now. Enhancing your self-esteem and reclaiming your inner strength and external power.

4. If you need to, this is a good week to seek healing. Choose a healer and a process that suits you and with whom you are prepared to work with. Healing is a two-way process and you must be a part of that process.

5. In the final analysis, strength lies in your attitude. As an adult you are now responsible for your attitude, your thoughts, your words and your actions. What has happened to you in the past cannot be changed. What can change is your attitude and how you approach each and every day. Look forward to better experiences and enjoy each moment to the fullest.

Week 35

Personal Challenges

Along with physical and psychological challenges there are many other personal challenges that we have to deal with and may weaken our self-esteem.

There are social and environmental issues that affect our lives. Where we live may have an impact on our attitude. There are the issues of unwanted or excess noise, traffic, pollution, government regulations, neighbours and other distractions that may cause distress. Often moving to a new location is not an option. In these circumstances we need to view these challenges as part of life's journey. Do what you can to alleviate the annoying aspects, yet accept them as lessons in patience, tolerance and empathy. Look at these challenges as part of a process to strengthen your self-esteem and not to diminish it.

Money may be another issue. For many people, money has an enormous effect on their self-esteem. For some, a plentiful supply of money enhances their self-esteem. In some cases it does not seem to matter if the cash is gained legally or illegally. For others, a lack of money is demoralizing. It is important to see money for what it is. Money and material possessions are a part of our life's journey. Money is like health, happiness, opportunity, friendship and other aspects of our human existence. Value them in the good times and accept and work through the challenges in the difficult times.

Finally, understand and accept who you are. None of us are perfect. Accept that there are situations and characteristics that you cannot change. Understand who you are and determine what you can change for your benefit and for the benefit of others. Life is challenging but we have chosen the experience. Use the experience and use it wisely.

Week 35

Exercises

1. Make a list of seven things that are important to you. They may be family, friendship, leisure, relaxation, another job, finding a partner, business success, expressing your creativity, more money, a holiday; the list is endless. You are to choose one of these for each day of this week.

2. After choosing one of these topics, spend at least ten minutes, writing down ways, how this desire can be fulfilled. Examine each of the possibilities. If there are possibilities that can be activated, do so. Others may need further investigation and planning. If that is the case, then accept the current situation, but plan for change and begin the process.

3. Whatever you choose to focus on each day, use a positive affirmation to reinforce that desire. For example, if you have a holiday as one of your important issues, you may affirm, "I have the necessary money and documentation to holiday in Paris." Always be specific in your affirmation. Always affirm in the positive. Always affirm in the present.

4. Remember this is not an exercise in wishful thinking. This is an exercise in taking action. If you desire to travel to Paris then make plans to do so. Begin saving. Check out the cost of flights. Collect travel brochures and talk to a travel agent. Plan your trip, complete with accommodation and itinerary.

5. Have an expectation that your situation will improve. Remember, though, action is needed and so is patience and endurance. Understand that not all things will come at once, but be grateful for the changes that do occur, and give yourself praise and credit, along with any other people who have assisted you. Also remember to stay determined and focused.

Week 36

Affirmations

The most effective means of maintaining and strengthening your self-esteem is by keeping everything about you in the positive and in the present.

This includes your thinking, your self-talk, your speech, your body language, your actions and your habits. All of these things define who you are. The more often you can make these things in the present and in the positive the stronger your self-esteem becomes.

Affirmations are a great tool in changing your patterns of behaviour into the positive and in to the present.

Affirmations may be formal or informal. In my archetype workshops we look at the archetype or the area of our life that this archetype dominates and examine what needs to be changed. We do this by ceasing to operate on the negative energy of that archetype and take up the positive energy. One of the ways we do this is to create a positive affirmation using the positive energy of the archetype. This is a formal affirmation. It is made in the present and in the positive. It is to be used many times throughout the day.

Other affirmations can be used in an informal way. If you are criticized in a negative way you can automatically change that to the positive. For example, if someone says you are irresponsible, you change that immediately to, "I am responsible and I decide what I do."

Use affirmations continuously. Always keep them in the present and not in the future. Discard words like 'when', 'if only', 'one day' and similar words or phrases. Always keep your affirmations in the positive. Affirmations work.

Week 36

Exercises

1. This is the week where you adopt the good habit of affirmations. Affirmations must always be in the present and the positive. Affirmations are most effective when they are relevant, succinct and short in length. Most of your affirmations will begin with, 'I am'. Affirmations can be used at any time and in all situations. Whatever your affirmation of the day is, just say it whenever it comes into your consciousness.

2. Choose three affirmations that you will focus on for the week. Make the first of these affirmations a statement that enhances one of your strengths, talents or qualities. For example, if you are a teacher, your first affirmation may be, "I am an excellent, dedicated teacher." This affirmation may be said whenever you are in a teaching situation or whenever you have a brief intellectual moment.

3. Make the second affirmation about an aspect of you that you are changing for the better. For example, if you are short-tempered and you are working on your level of patience, affirm, "I am patient and tolerant in all situations."

4. Make the third affirmation about a person, situation or event that elicits stress, fear or negativity. This could apply to several people and to a variety of situations. Affirm, "I am calm, brave and never deal in negativity." This type of affirmation is essential when some person or occasion is pushing your stress, fear or negativity buttons. Affirm and then sing your favourite song. This type of affirmation should also be used when you are relaxed and feel good about yourself. The purpose of all affirmations is to strengthen you in the good times as well as dealing with the challenging times.

Week 37

Get Rid of the Clutter

For many of us our lives are full to the brim with responsibilities, obligations and expectations. When we do get a chance for rest and recreation we take it with open arms. Time is speeding up and we are expected to keep up with the change. There are occasions when we can be overwhelmed with all that is happening and all that is expected.

We have talked about establishing your priorities and your involvement in nothing else but those priorities. This allows you to focus on what is really important to you. It also allows you to rid yourself of situations and things that are of no value to you anymore.

It pays to have a physical clean-out. Look at all those possessions that you have not used for many years and donate them to a person or organization that will use them.

Once you begin cleaning out the clutter you allow space for more relevant things to enter your life.

Removing the physical clutter is important. Removing the mental clutter is equally important. A technique called 'morning pages' is especially beneficial. For those of you who possess a Philosopher or Seeker archetype and when your mind is always full of questions or if you have trouble making decisions then 'morning pages' is essential.

When you first wake, you take your pen and paper and write. Do not think about what you write, just write. Write at least one page, preferably two. You do not need to re-read your pages. You can keep them or discard them. 'Morning pages' removes the mental clutter and the good ideas that come can be put into practice.

Week 37

Exercises

1. Begin with what is inside your home. Choose a room, Sit quietly and look around the room. See if there is anything in that room that has lost its meaning or that is just taking up space, serving no useful purpose and having no value to you either sentimentally or emotionally. Take it out of the room and give it away.

2. Go to your wardrobe and chest of drawers and carefully assess all of your clothing and footwear. Cull all those items that you rarely wear or have not worn for a very long time. Never use the excuse of, "I will wear it when I lose weight." We all know that when you lose weight, you will want to purchase new items. Make sure you inspect your shoes as well. Take all the items you do not need or want and give them to charity or dispose of them sensibly.

3. If you have children, check out all the items that are no longer used or needed. Leave their toys. If they choose to cull their toys, then that is a decision for them to make. You may encourage them but respect their needs and emotional attachments. However, baby changing tables, nappy holders, bouncinettes, high chairs, car seats, baby monitors, bassinets, basketball rings and other sporting gear that are no longer used need to go. Once again give them away or dispose of them sensibly.

4. Take a quiet moment and consider your friends. Are there any friends who fill your relationship with constant demands, neediness or negativity? The time has come to cut them loose. This can be done gently and over time but this is the time to begin the process.

5. As you cull the various items, consider what you want to replace those items you have disposed of. Once you create a vacuum it will certainly be filled in a short space of time. It is better to fill it with what you want or need rather than more stuff that is just going to replace one lot of clutter with a different lot of clutter.

Week 38

Meditation

'Morning pages' is a great technique and a good starting point for those people who have trouble stilling their mind. If you are capable of stilling your mind then move into meditation.

Meditation not only stills your mind and relaxes you but also puts you in touch with your spiritual self.

There are some people who can meditate on a regular basis and for a good length of time. This is an advantage. These individuals will understand the benefits of their meditation.

If you are a beginner or if you meditate on an irregular basis then keep persisting. There are many things that are worth the effort and meditation is one of them.

Find a meditation that suits you. In the beginning it may be worthwhile for you to go to a venue and be lead on your meditation by a facilitator. Always go to a place and a facilitator where you feel comfortable.

If you wish to meditate at home or in your own environment, then that is the way to go. There are many audio meditations available. Find the ones that suit you. You may stay with the same guided meditation or you may change. There are no set rules. Meditate according to your mood and your intention.

After a while you may wish and be capable of organizing your own meditation. You may wish to meditate upon one particular subject or you may feel like accepting whatever the universe gives you. Once again there are no set rules. You decide.

Week 38

Exercises

1. This is the time to begin, re-visit or continue the practice of meditation. Make your meditation a daily event. If you can take yourself to a centre for a daily meditation that is an ideal situation. However, for most people this is impractical, so a home meditation is usually more suited to our responsibilities and commitments. If you are restricted or feel more comfortable at home, that is fine. Set aside at least half an hour for your meditation. Make sure you can meditate at a time and in a space where there are no distractions. There are plenty of guided meditations that you can use. If you are happy to meditate without a guided meditation then choose a subject for your meditation.

    The key is to meditate. If you have difficulty in meditating, and a lot of people do, stay firm and resolute. To still your mind, even briefly, is beneficial to your well-being. Meditate with commitment. Even if you lead a busy life, set aside some time for meditation and do this happily and without feeling guilty that you should be doing some other chore. Slot a regular time into your daily routine and commit. The challenge of meditation is worth the reward.

Week 39

Visualization

The importance of living in the present and in the positive cannot be overlooked. Most of the techniques for maintaining and enhancing self-esteem rely on working in the present.

However, it is also important to plan for the future. The key is to make planning for the future realistic and to take action.

Visualization is a worthy technique. Placing a picture in your mind or in your environment and focusing on that image to bring it to reality is fine so long as you obey the rules.

There will be many examples where the rules have not been observed and the visualization fails. Placing a photo of the new sports car or an image of you twenty kilograms lighter on the refrigerator door is only a first step. There is no fairy godmother that will come along and wave her magic wand and present you with the sports car or a slimmer, lighter body.

Always make sure that the object of your visualization is realistic and attainable within a short time frame. Commitment and hard work is required to achieve a goal over a long time frame. Gaining tertiary qualifications is a three or four year long term commitment. It is a process that we undergo. Visualization has a shorter time frame expectation.

The sports car may need to be a cheaper model. The weight loss can be lowered to five kilograms. Then, follow the visualization with action. Begin to save for the car. Change your diet and start an exercise program. It is important to realize your visualization. Each success enhances self-esteem, failure lowers self-esteem.

Week 39

Exercises

1. Every day spend some time visualizing. Set aside a few minutes for your visualization. Begin your meditation with visualization. Whenever you have some quiet time, remain still and visualize. This may only be for a matter of a few seconds. Even that amount of time is important, as it continually reinforces what you are striving for.

2. Ensure that the subject of your visualization is relevant and realistic. Re-visit your priorities or goals and choose a change or an achievement that is currently very important to you. Create an image in your mind. Ensure that the image is on the final product and not on the process. Bring your attention to this image throughout the week.

3. Keep your focus on a limited number of visualizations. Your energy needs to remain focused and not diffused. If you can, restrict yourself to one image or visualization and certainly no more than three.

4. Remember that visualization is not wishful thinking. What you are visualizing is the end product of action. Visualization is a waste of your time and energy if you fail to take action. The process of change and achievement is a combination of thought, word and action.

Week 40

One Step at a Time

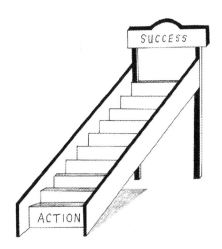

We are constantly faced with a world that says you are entitled to instant manifestation and gratification. Buy now and use your credit card. Take advantage of our 'no interest loans'. Lose weight and get the figure you desire by drinking our special weight-loss formula. The media is full of images and promises of your entitlement.

All of this emotional advertising and imagery plays upon your self-esteem. You will look great. You will feel better. You deserve it. This becomes the land of fantasy and, of course, your ego loves to be there. Then reality hits. Your self-esteem understands reality. Your self-esteem knows exactly where you are.

Enhancing your self-esteem is not a product of fantasy. Enhancing your self-esteem is the result of conscious understanding, changing your attitude and of living in the present and the positive.

With your self-esteem, success builds upon success. It is important to be successful. Therefore, be realistic, be prepared to work and always take one step at a time.

When we attempt too much, the task becomes overwhelming and we set ourselves up for failure. We tell ourselves that we are a failure and our self-esteem takes a hit. Sometimes, others tell us about our failures and, once again, our self-esteem takes a hit.

When you progress one step at a time, each success builds upon the previous achievement. Even when something goes wrong you can look back and see what has been achieved. This gives you the confidence to diverge to plan B but to continue on your quest.

Week 40

Exercises

1. Write down 2 aspects of your life that you wish to change or 2 goals that you would like to reach. The first aspect or goal should be a minor task that is achievable within this week. Keep it simple and keep it doable. There are many things that fit into these criteria. Here are a few possibilities. You may desire to lose 2 kilograms in weight. What about changing your diet to a healthier intake of food. You may decide to cut back on your smoking or drinking. Maybe there is a room in your house that needs redecorating or a patch of garden that needs a facelift. Is there a creative project that has been neglected or put aside but may be finished with some effort and attention?

2. When you have decided on your minor task, write down a seven step process that will achieve your aim. If your choice is to lose weight, write down an action for each day that will assist with achieving this goal. On day one, you may decide to fast. On day two, you may decide to eat only salads. On day three, you may decide to eliminate all alcohol and soft drinks. When you have decided on your seven step program, put it into action.

3. When you have decided on your major task, write down a seven step process that will achieve your aim. As this task is more of a challenge, the aim is to achieve a result in seven weeks. Allow yourself one week to achieve each of the seven steps. The key is to keep the task achievable within a seven week timeframe. Finishing a creative project should fit in nicely with this timeframe. Renovating a room would also suit. Changing your diet is another option. For example, in week one, every day have a salad for lunch, cut out bread, drink only water, go without sugar, eliminate take-away meals or fried food. You may choose an easy option for week one and keep the more difficult choices for weeks six and seven. By then you will be determined to succeed and with the achievement of one task, the second task will not look so daunting.

Week 41

Two Steps Forward, One Step Back

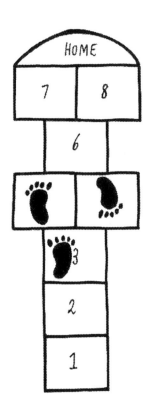

Life was never designed to be a journey of smooth sailing. There will always be obstacles and challenges. These are a part of the life experience. Then, of course, there is human nature. We are human with all our amazing attributes and all our frailties and weaknesses.

Even with the most pure of intentions and stern resolve we are bound to make mistakes or fall into negative behaviours. We need to recognize that this is part of our journey. When we recognize our mistakes and any negative behaviour patterns we can begin to change. Learn the lessons and move on into positive behaviour patterns.

Living life in the present and the positive and enhancing our self-esteem is a process of two steps forward and one step backwards. The key is to recognize and acknowledge when we are progressing and when we fall.

Always give yourself credit for progress. Compliment and praise yourself on a job well done or on the righteous decisions you have made. Accept the compliments of others and the rewards that are offered. Do this with humility and satisfaction. This strengthens your self-esteem. This gives you encouragement to continue with positive and present patterns of behaviours. This gives you the confidence to transfer your skills and positive behaviours into other areas of your life.

If you do fall back into a negative pattern of behaviour then stop, reflect and change. Never feel guilty. Recognize the behaviour and change back to the present and the positive.

Week 41

Exercises

1. Every night this week take five minutes to reflect on the day's events. Write down the occasions when you have involved yourself in negativity. The negativity may have been directed towards yourself, another person or with an event. Consider if you changed that initial negativity into a positive. If you did that compliment yourself. If your attitude stayed in the negative consider a different course of reaction or behaviour that would have changed the situation into a positive experience.

2. Continue this process every night. Look for negative patterns of behaviour. Are you involving yourself with the same negative behaviour on a consistent basis? Is there a person who continually presses your buttons? Is there a situation or commitment that places you under stress? Are your thought patterns or self-talk steeped in negativity towards certain situations? Are you repeating the same mistake on a regular basis? Examine the challenge and look for the solution. Check your attitude. Are you being reactive and can you be proactive? Is it possible to avoid certain people, places or events? Are you in control of your emotions or do your emotions control you?

3. At the end of the week collect your writings that list all your negative occasions. Burn them. Burn every one of them. If you are so inclined you may conduct a small ceremony to mark the occasion. Affirm the positive behaviour. For example, if stealing from your work place was the issue, burn your recordings of these events. Then affirm, "I am honest. I never steal." In the future, every time you are tempted, you affirm, "I am honest. I never steal."

Week 42

Taking Time for You

One of the most important exercises in enhancing your self-esteem is to take some time for yourself. This needs to be done on a regular and consistent basis.

As adults we have many responsibilities and commitments that we often lose a part of our identity. There are also adventures and experiences that have eluded us. The idea of taking time for yourself is to give you permission to be you, to have experiences that were denied to you and for your psychological well-being.

Begin by listening to your inner child. Your Child archetype has the most amazing innocence, wisdom and spirit of adventure. Your inner child may suggest that you go for a walk in the bush. Do so. Would you like to make mud pies, paint a picture, take in a movie, go dancing, surround yourself with animals or swim in the ocean? Do whatever feels right for you. There were many things that we were denied as children or that were discouraged. As adults we have the control and the resources to engage in those missed, simple pleasures. There may also be adventures that we would love to re-visit. The choice is yours.

The key is that time for yourself is time alone. This is not a date with your partner. This is not a social occasion with a friend. This is not a family gathering. This is time spent by you, for you.

Put aside at least an hour each and every week. Keep this time regular. For example, every Sunday evening from eight o'clock to ten o'clock is your time. If people and events need to be organized for this to happen, then do so. This is your time, enjoy it.

Week 42

Exercises

1. This is the week to spend some time on you. Every day do something for you. It may be something very simple or it may be an immense pleasure you have been putting off for a while. Allow yourself whatever time it takes and work that time into your schedule. The time needed may be five minutes or it may be an hour. You could relax in a bath. You could treat yourself to a massage. You could take a walk or go for a swim. You could relax and watch a film you have been waiting to see. The choice is yours. However, choose something that you find difficult to fit into your daily life or something that you enjoy doing but haven't done for many months.

2. Make a list of activities that you enjoy. Consider this list and write down the frequency of your participation in each of these activities. Are you content with your leisure time? Do your responsibilities and your leisure overlap? Are you devoting all of your leisure time on the demands or requests of others? Is it possible to fit some of these activities into your life without compromising your responsibilities or commitments? Do your leisure activities reflect your passion or do you just accept what comes along?

3. Give yourself permission to choose and to participate in leisure activities. This is not a case of being selfish. This is a case of taking care of your psychological and emotional well-being. This is a case of looking after your self-esteem. Remember, there is a huge difference in allowing you some me-time and totally selfish self-indulgence.

Week 43

Responsibility

Responsibility is such a dynamic word. It may mean different things to different people. It may evoke various emotional responses. It is certainly one of life's lessons that we can embrace, accept with ambivalence or try to ignore.

From the perspective of your self-esteem, responsibility means understanding you and being accountable for your thoughts, words and actions.

As a functioning adult, you are responsible for you. You are responsible for your thoughts, words and deeds. You are in charge of your emotions. You are in charge of your attitudes.

If you want to permanently enhance and strengthen your self-esteem you need to take up the challenge of responsibility.

It is easy to blame your parents for your attitudes. "This is what my parents taught me." So are you, you or are you, your parents? You choose your attitude and your parents choose theirs.

It is easy to blame the system or the society for your situation. "This is what is expected." "The government doesn't look after me." You are the person making decisions for you. Enjoy what is given to you with humility and gratitude and never with entitlement.

It is easy to blame others for your negative emotions. "My boss makes me so angry." Your boss may be negative, demanding, out-of-touch or many other things but you decide if you get angry. Your boss may not even notice. You are in charge of your attitudes, thoughts, words, deeds and emotions, nobody else.

Week 43

Exercises

1. These exercises may be the most challenging. If you stumble and fall back into negative habits, then remember, two steps forward and one step back is still good progress. Maintain your determination and your resilience. Keep guilt at bay. Continue to be aware of your thoughts, words and actions and keep affirming in the positive and in the present.

2. Keep your word. If you say you are going to do something, then do it. If you say you will ring a friend tomorrow evening, then phone them. If you say you will take a neighbour shopping, then it is important to take your neighbour shopping. If a person needs your help and you say you will be there in ten minutes, then be there in ten minutes. Keep your word. If you are asked for help and you cannot be of service then say so. Only commit when you are able. If something does crop up, then communicate what has happened and if needed make another time. This week, focus on keeping your word. That is taking up the challenge of responsibility.

Week 44

Balance

Balance is an important issue when it comes to self-esteem. Self-esteem does not rely upon success in one area of our lives. Yes, success is important. Success boosts our self-esteem.

However, we are not one-dimensional personalities. There are many examples of top sports people, pop icons or film stars who lack balance. No doubt their success temporarily strengthens their self-esteem. Yet, within a short time period, their unbalanced lives weakens their self-esteem and they fall into disrepute or unable to cope in other areas.

Addiction is similar in nature. No matter what the addiction, the individual involved lacks balance. All their attention becomes focused on the next hit offered by the addiction.

Balance is about participation. Your life's journey is about the learning experiences. When you are involved with work, family, friends, leisure or creativity, you are empowering yourself in so many ways and strengthening your self-esteem. Your self-esteem ensures a 'can-do' attitude and exudes confidence which permeates so many aspects of your life.

Balance is also about the acknowledgement that life is riddled with challenges and setbacks. If our self-esteem is strong, if we have balance and a strong attitude in other aspects of our life, we accept these challenges and setbacks with determination and positivity. We become resilient. We learn our lessons. We strengthen our resolve.

Balance encourages a positive attitude to all aspects of our life. Self-esteem is multi-dimensional and balance is paramount.

Week 44

Exercises

1. Take the time to write down how many hours you spend at work, how many hours you spend resting and how many hours you spend at leisure. If you are at home, housekeeping or caring for your children, that is considered work. Is your life in balance? Are you spending so many hours at work that it diminishes your time for rest and leisure? You may not be able to change that situation in the short term, so it is important that you have quality rest and leisure time. It is also a situation that needs consideration into your future planning. If you are in the fortunate position of having an ample amount of leisure time, then consider how that time is used. Leisure time is for enjoyment and relaxation. However, always consider how you can use your leisure time to be more productive.

2. One of the great benefits of knowing and understanding your archetypes is that they give you an understanding of how balanced your life is. For example, if you have an Artist archetype then you constantly need a creative project, either in the planning stage or the production stage. Therefore, look at your creative side. Are you frustrated that your life is full of responsibility and you haven't allocated time to spend on your creative pursuits? Are you the Adventurer who needs time outdoors and exploring nature? Are you the Athlete or the Warrior and you no longer allow yourself time for sport or physical activity? Consider who you are and what activities you enjoy. If there is an activity that you are missing, work it back into your schedule. Balance encourages a healthy lifestyle, a strong mental attitude and an enhanced self-esteem.

3. On, at least one occasion this week, participate in an activity that you have not attempted before. This does not have to be a life-changing experience. It may be something rather simple. Life is a journey of adventure. Enjoy each experience, new or old.

Week 45

Worry

The one guaranteed way to weaken our self-esteem is to worry. Worry saps our energy. Worry distracts us. Worry erodes our confidence. Worry leads to stress. Worry diverts our attitude from the things we can do to the things that challenge us. Worry weakens our self-esteem.

It is so important for our self-esteem to eliminate worry from our lives. This, of course, is easier said than done. However, it is important to deal with the habit of worry.

Let us differentiate worry from the term 'concerned with'. Worry is when you are emotionally involved in a process. This process may be real or it may be imagined. Worry is constantly thinking about a challenge, what has happened or what may happen. Worry takes away your focus from so many other aspects of your daily living.

On the other hand, 'being concerned with' means that you are dealing with matters that are important. 'Being concerned with', means taking action. If a bill needs payment, there is little use in worrying about it. It is however important to be concerned and take action. Pay the bill. If money is tight, seek support from a friend or negotiate a plan for payment options.

So much of what we worry about never happens. Worry does not differentiate between the important issues and the minor aspects of life. The rule says, "If the issues are important in twelve months then take action and deal with them. If they are not important in twelve months' time then ignore them."

When you follow this rule, worry quickly disappears.

Week 45

Exercises

1. Your first exercise this week is to sit down, relax and write down all the things you worry about. Place a number besides each item. If they are small or minor in nature, then place a 1 beside them. If the worries are large or major in nature, then place a 2 beside them.

2. Let us deal with the minor worries. Ask yourself this question. "Is there anything you can do to change the situation?" If the answer is yes, then take action and eliminate the worry. If the answer is no, then we have to consider the rationality of worrying. When there is no logical reason to worry, there is usually fear involved. For example, you may be afraid of dogs. Deal with this issue. Call a friend who has a dog, preferably a big, friendly dog. Meet your friend at a neutral venue as some dogs are protective of their home environment especially with nervous strangers. Walk the dog together. Visit a dog park. Once you relax the dogs will completely ignore you. They are more concerned with other dogs. Once you have established that core calmness and strength, the fear of dogs will diminish. The worry will disappear.

3. After we have dealt with the minor worries, move on to the major issues. Understand that these may take longer to solve but begin the process with strength and determination. Once again consider the logic of your worry. Is it an irrational fear? If it is a major psychological fear, such as a fear of heights, claustrophobia or fear of flying you may be better off seeking professional assistance. The alternative is to live with that fear and, for example, never fly. If you are still determined to rid yourself of this worry and a professional is not the answer then work on changing your attitude and affirming a positive outcome.

Week 46

Stress

Stress is even more debilitating than worry. Stress damages self-esteem. Stress affects our health and general well-being. Stress causes us to lose balance and perspective in our lives.

Constant worrying can lead to stress. Once you eliminate the habit of worrying, you can lessen the amount of stress that is placed upon you.

However, there are other causes of stress. Taking on too much, making a number of difficult commitments, pressure from work, family or friends, health and safety issues may all cause stress.

The process to alleviate stress is similar to the one that alleviates worry. However, the intensity is different, as stress is a more intense emotion. So, the answer is to be concerned and take action.

The first step with being concerned about stress is awareness. Be aware of your lifestyle. Is your lifestyle in balance or do you focus on one particular issue? Alternatively, are you involved in so many issues that there is little time left for you? Once you are aware of your lifestyle then you are able to focus on balance.

Eliminate some of the unnecessary activities. Cut down on the time-consuming, major activities that causes stress. You may need to examine your work commitment, your relationships, your diet, and your exercise or leisure regime.

The key is awareness followed by action. Be aware of those things that cause stress. Take action to change. Lessen or eliminate stress and take greater care of your self-esteem.

Week 46

Exercises

1. Every day this week, before you go to sleep, write down the occasions during that day when you felt that you were under stress. Also, write down what was the cause of that stress. Determine if the cause of your stress was self-induced or as a result of external factors. With both internal and external causes, you can work on your attitude. There are a number of things you can put into place.

    (a) Whatever issue caused your stress, decide on the importance of the issue. Will it be a challenge in a week's time? Begin to evaluate what is important and what is trivial. Discernment is the key. When you practice discernment, you learn to ignore or let go of trivial matters that are likely to cause stress.

    (b) Can you avoid the people, situations or events that cause you stress? This seems a fairly obvious course of action, yet, through some misguided concept of loyalty, weakness, duty, guilt or the whole range of emotions and social conventions, we feel that we have to put ourselves through torturous relationships or events. Only attend events that demand your presence. Interact with negative people only when it is imperative to interact. Avoid situations that cause you stress.

    (c) When it is absolutely necessary to interact in potentially stressful situations, affirm your confidence and ability to deal with this situation. Affirm, "I am confident and up to this challenge."

    (d) Avoid conflicts, arguments and discussions that cause you stress. We all know that there are some topics, especially religion and politics, which should never be discussed in the company of some people. It takes two people to argue. Be firm. Be polite. Ask a question then change the subject.

2. Every day this week engage yourself in meditation, yoga, tai chi or some similar activity that will focus your attention away from the issues that cause stress and into a state of relaxation.

Week 47

Empathy

A very important human attribute to have is the attribute of empathy. Empathy gives us a connection with both our humanity and spirituality.

Empathy is not the same as sympathy. Sympathy is full of emotion. Sympathy is to feel sorrow for another or for a situation. Sympathy is a human characteristic. Empathy is the ability to understand and enter into another's experience. This is not just a feeling but a deep knowledge and understanding of another's situation or experience. Empathy is both a human and spiritual characteristic.

Remember our self-esteem is an attitude not merely an emotion. Empathy reflects this attitude. Our attitude to ourselves is reflected in our attitude to others. If your self-esteem is low and you do not regard yourself as worthy in various aspects of your life then it is likely that you will regard others in the same light. For example, if your attitude to your job suggests that your contribution is mundane, your skills and effort are not appreciated or this job is not what you wanted, you are more likely to be dissatisfied, not only within yourself, but also with the boss, fellow workers and the work routine and responsibilities. The whole experience becomes a vicious circle. The dissatisfaction in your job fuels the dissatisfaction with who you are and what you are doing with your life. It keeps your self-esteem down at a low level.

Empathy allows an appreciation of others no matter if their situation is better or worse than your situation. This appreciation flows on to an appreciation of who you are and what you do. An appreciation of yourself enhances your self-esteem.

Week 47

Exercises

1. Watch the news, a television show or a film and choose one of the people or characters that are going through challenging times. You could just as easily choose a friend or acquaintance. Write a short letter to them indicating how they could help themselves and how you could assist them in getting through the challenging times.

2. Place yourself in the position of this other person and read your advice. How would you feel and would you follow that advice. Feel free to do this exercise several times during the week.

3. Choose a person who is a challenge for you to deal with. Every day this week, take 30 seconds of your time and send this person your love. Imagine sending them pink balloons filled with love that pop just above their head and shower them with small droplets of love.

4. Message a person who you haven't contacted in a while. Just say hello and ask them how they are travelling. The message should be short and simple. Expect no reply.

5. Consider the harshest punishment or treatment that you would inflict on another. Place yourself in this person's shoes. Would you still be willing to go through with this punishment if the other person was your partner, your son or your daughter?

Week 48

Honesty

Honesty is a huge discipline. There are so many aspects of our humanity and our civilization that encourages and rewards dishonesty and punishes honesty. There are times when our personal self-protection devices encourage us to lie and not be honest. There are many social or friendship situations that exist through a veil of deceit and deception. Every day we are bombarded with dishonesty from our leaders through to advertising and personal relationships.

The situation is confused and compounded when, as children, we are told by both parents and teachers to be honest. We have a legal system that seeks and depends on honesty. Yet we are surrounded with deception.

Is it any wonder that our self-esteem suffers?

Yet honesty is so important in the long-term and permanent strengthening of our self-esteem. Dishonesty is a protective measure and a short-term high. Honesty is a long-term strength.

So, begin with, being honest with yourself. Tell yourself the truth. If you steal from your work place, you are a thief. Cease the stealing and you are honest. This is a negative example. There are also positive examples where you lie to yourself. If you have achieved a goal or completed a task really well, never dismiss it as something simple or of no consequence. Be honest and give yourself credit and praise.

When you are honest with yourself you can be honest with others. Honesty enables you to be pure in your thoughts, your words and your actions. Honest relationships are a joy to all parties, never a burden.

Week 48

Exercises

1. Be honest. If something does not belong to you, then it is not yours to take. Be honest and leave it where it belongs. Do this all week and congratulate yourself for your honesty.

2. Every day and on multiple occasions affirm, "I am honest. I never steal."

3. When you are tempted to take something that is not yours, even if it is just a pen from your workplace, leave it where it is and affirm, "I am honest. I never steal."

4. Monitor your thoughts, your words and your actions. Are you honest with yourself or do you justify and excuse your dishonesty? Never believe that because others engage in dishonesty that it gives you an excuse for your dishonesty. It is a similar situation with large businesses and corporations. Never excuse yourself with thoughts such as "They can afford it." They won't miss it." This is no excuse for stealing. "I deserve it" is another common excuse. There is also the justification of, "they stole from me so I can steal from them." That makes you dishonest. That brings you down to the same level and using the same negative energy. From now on, there are no excuses or justifications for stealing. Be honest.

Week 49

Truth

Honesty and truth are very similar in nature. You are free to classify them as the same. However, from the point of view of strengthening your self-esteem, let us consider that honesty is a specific attribute and that truth is the overriding virtue.

Being both honest and truthful in all situations is never easy. It is a task that is continually testing our awareness, our resolve and our personality traits. That is why we need to be constantly aware of our thoughts, our words and our actions.

It is also important to understand that truth and perception may not be the same thing. Understand that how you perceive situations, events and relationships may not be totally truthful in essence. This is where empathy enters as a balancing tool. By all means look at things from your perspective but understand that another will be looking at the same thing through their eyes. This is personal perception. The truth may be something different from either person's perception.

Despite our personal perceptions we should always be seeking the truth and be truthful in all our dealings.

Please remember that being truthful is not a tool for revenge. For example, if you disagree with someone never resort to personal insults even though what you say may be the truth. Truth is to be used with caring and compassion.

Being truthful is being true to your word and to your positive self. Truth is to be positive. Positivity enhances self-esteem.

Week 49

Exercises

1. Tell the truth. This week there is to be no excuses and no lies. Whatever you are responsible for, take ownership of that responsibility. If you make a mistake, say so. If something wasn't done and it was your responsibility, then admit the truth. No more passing the blame onto others. Remember, that telling the truth is not an excuse for revenge. If you have information about another's deceit, there is no excuse to use that information for the purposes of revenge. Telling the truth is a positive habit. Revenge is a negative habit. You can tell the truth and still be discerning.

2. Begin with telling the truth to yourself. This does not have to be an admission of your failures or personal condemnation of your actions. The last thing you should do is to send yourself on a guilt trip. This is an honest assessment of your thoughts and what you say to yourself. Check to see if you are deluding yourself. If there is falsification, then correct the record in a positive way. For example, if you consider yourself a safe driver but have a history of penalties, admit the truth. Affirm, "I always drive according to the road rules." As another example look at your diet. If you consider yourself to have a healthy diet and then proceed to consume processed and take-away food for the majority of your meals, then admit the truth. Again, the purpose of this exercise is not to make you feel guilty. The purpose is to come to terms with the truth. If you wish to change your dietary habits, then take action. Eat fresh food and affirm your new positive eating habits.

3. When you have come to terms with being honest with yourself you can begin to be honest with others. Always affirm, "I am an honest person who always tells the truth." As mentioned before, be discerning. This is not an exercise in telling everyone's secrets. However, it is an exercise in talking openly and honestly but with compassion and discernment.

Week 50

Courage

Being courageous enhances self-esteem. Being courageous gives you a sense of identity. Being courageous gives you permission to take risks. Being courageous encourages achievement.

Courage expands your world and experience. Courage allows for risk-taking. Fear inhibits your world and experience. Fear allows for excuses.

Be aware of your definition of courage. Courage means that you face all of life's experiences with positivity and affirmative action.

Life is full of rewards and challenges. Courage allows you to rejoice and appreciate the joys of life. This is important to understand. Appreciate and give thanks for the good times. Have the courage to admit that life is rewarding, even when engaging in some of the most mundane of tasks.

Courage also allows you to accept and deal with the challenges of life. Some challenges will be small in nature while others will be immense. Be positive in your attitude and face each one with confidence in your ability, and courage in your determination.

We all know and understand that there will be challenges. Some take more resolve than others. However, it is your attitude and your courage that determines how well you meet and deal with each challenge.

The stronger your self-esteem, the more capable you are to deal with life's challenges. As you conquer one challenge your self-esteem will be enhanced and you know you can face another challenge with both courage and confidence.

Week 50

Exercises

1. Every day this week affirm, "I face life's challenges with courage."

2. Change at least one aspect of your daily routine. You could take a different way to work. You could turn off the television and, with your family, play a board game. Maybe you could draw or paint or involve yourself with a creative activity. There are a myriad of groups you could join. Harness your courage and do something different. If you do not like the change in your routine then return to the old routine.

3. Consider one fear that challenges you consistently. Choose a fear that you generally have to face and not one that you can easily avoid. Let us use the fear of loneliness as an example. Take steps to overcome that fear. Affirm, "I always have friends that support and surround me." At least once a week make the effort to take yourself out of your house. If you do not drive then check out the local community transport situation. Join a group. Volunteer at a local organization. Take up the challenge to overcome this fear with a courageous attitude and action.

4. When dealing with your challenges remember to take them on one at a time. When dealing with challenges, the more control you have the less overwhelmed you become. For some people, there are various challenges that can be dealt with by a decision and an attitude change. For example, to give up smoking, there comes a point when various individuals decide they will no longer smoke. They make a decision. They summon their courage and mental strength. They change their attitude and affirm, "I am healthy and have no need to smoke." As an incentive they place all their cigarette money in a jar. This is an ideal way to face a challenge. However, there are other challenges that require a step by step progression. For example, dealing with grief requires a steady and courageous approach. Keep affirming and courageously deal with one day at a time.

Week 51

Resilience

One of humanity's most enduring and positive characteristics is resilience.

Resilience is strength. Resilience is perseverance. Resilience is determination. Resilience is our ability to bounce back from any setback, small or large, and to continue life with passion and positivity.

Resilience is such an important attribute to strengthen and maintain our self-esteem. Our self-esteem is never static. Our self-esteem changes from situation to situation and from day to day. The variation of our self-esteem differs from person to person and changes constantly in each one of us.

If your self-esteem stays on a relatively steady course then resilience plays only a minor role. However, if your self-esteem moves up and down frequently or if you suffer long periods of self-doubt and poor self-esteem then resilience plays a vital role in lifting you out of the doldrums and back into balance.

There are other occasions when, no matter how strong your self-esteem may be, you will succumb. You may question yourself. Your confidence dissipates. You become emotionally vulnerable. The death of a family member or of a close friend, a relationship break-up, a severe accident, losing your home or job or a significant financial loss are all events can dent your self-esteem.

This is when you need to call upon all of your resilience. Resilience pushes you through the pain and discomfort. Resilience gives you hope that life will get better and you will return to your true self, stronger and with a positive attitude.

Week 51

Exercises

1. Find some quiet time and recall several times when life's challenges became overwhelming or difficult to deal with. Consider and think through each process. Write down how you worked your way through each challenge. Was it a day-by-day process? Did you make a decision to keep on keeping on and battle your way through the crisis? Did you receive professional help? Did you call upon family or friends to assist you? Did you struggle through all alone or did you accept assistance? Did you throw yourself into a project? Did you withdraw from the world to renew and regenerate? Have you accepted that some challenges are ongoing and may be with you for the rest of your life?

2. Write down your attributes or personality traits that assisted you when dealing with these challenges. They may include mental toughness, stubbornness, conviction, love, dedication, determination, strength, courage, surrender, acceptance, sense of duty, or many others. List the attributes that you use on a regular basis. Make an affirmation for each one. For example, "I am determined to face each challenge with courage and resolve."

3. When confronted with a challenge, always focus on your strong attributes and personality traits. Use them to bounce back from a setback. Call upon your resilience and these strong personality assets to protect you, to focus you and to push you through this challenge. Also affirm, "I am strong, I am resilient. I accept and defeat all challenges."

Week 52

Contentment

If you can see contentment as an attitude and not as an emotion your self-esteem will be impenetrable. When you are content your self-esteem will remain strong.

Contentment is an attitude that says that no matter what happens in my life I am satisfied with myself and I am living life to the fullest.

When you are following your passion, you can be content.

When you are experiencing a wonderful experience, you can be content.

When you are faced with a significant challenge, you can be content.

Contentment is that inner peace that gives you permission to be yourself and to lead the life that you choose or that which is presented to you or the combination of both.

Even if you do not have the job you would like, you can still be content with the job you have. Even if you would like your home to be grander and to have more modern appliances and furniture, you can still be content with the home you have. Even if you would like your children to be smarter or more polite, you can still find and focus on their good qualities.

This does not say to accept second-best. It does not say to never strive for something better. Contentment focuses on what you have, what you have achieved and gives you permission to strive for change and improvement. Remember, contentment is an attitude.

Week 52

Exercises

1. Every moment of every day, make sure you are aware of your level
    of contentment. Yes, contentment can be an emotion. However,
    more importantly, contentment is an attitude and a state of mind.
    Contentment is that inner peace that is so easily upset by our experiences
    and the people that surround us. When you are aware of your level
    of contentment, you can bring it to the fore no matter what your
    circumstances.

2. When you are feeling good about yourself. When you are on an emotional
    high. When you are involved in an activity that you are passionate
    about. When you have achieved success. Enjoy your emotions of joy,
    happiness, excitement, pride, satisfaction, exhilaration and the like.
    However, focus deeper than your emotions. Bring to the fore your level
    of contentment. This is a much quieter feeling. Contentment and inner
    peace is the knowledge and understanding of your personal strength
    and the utilization of your talents and abilities. Keep the memory of
    that inner peace and contentment continually strong in your psyche.

3. When you are challenged. When things do not go to plan. When you
    are feeling down or depressed. When people are annoying. When life
    is difficult. When you are angry, frustrated, annoyed, stressed and the
    like. Sit quietly. Tap into your inner peace and contentment. Focus on
    that feeling. Focus on your strengths, your talents and your abilities.
    Recall a time when you were proud and excited and recall how your
    contentment level resonated with you. Bring that attitude and that
    feeling into existence. Sit with it for a short time. Then, when you are in
    control and have that contentment level totally in your consciousness,
    take action to change whatever challenge you face.

About the Author

Brian Dale is an experienced primary school teacher, workshop facilitator, archetype consultant, author, storyteller, playwright, drama teacher and director.

In 2002, his insightful wife, Robyn, inspired him to be trained as an archetype consultant at the Australian Institute of Caroline Myss. Archetypes are universal personifications, such as, Princess, King, Priestess, Goddess, Knight, Victim, Warrior, Rescuer and many more.

"Archetypes are powerful tools that give you an understanding of your true self, how you can heal and how you can change and improve various aspects of your life."

Brian's intuition and insightful observations have assisted many people to fully understand themselves and their place in this physical world. He has facilitated archetype workshops throughout Australia and overseas. His knowledge of archetypes has given Brian an understanding of the importance of our Victim archetype which determines our self-esteem. Our self-esteem is the key archetypal energy that works with all other energies.

With the passing of his daughter, Tahla, Brian was taken in another direction. He was inspired to investigate the Afterlife. With the assistance of Tahla and her spirit guide, Simeon, Brian is able to pass on their messages and information about what happens to us when we depart from this physical world. This is outlined in the book 'Decoding the Afterlife'.

"This is a stimulating journey and I am relishing every step and every experience."

As a primary school teacher he has over 35 years' experience having taught in both public and private schools. Brian is a trained teacher-librarian and an entertaining storyteller. His storytelling led him into writing children's books. He is a published author and his stories for children have been used in standardized tests by both the Victorian and South Australian Education Departments.

One of his greatest passions is drama and performing arts. He is the co-founder of Bright Lights Performance School. Brian has written, produced and directed many Bright Lights performances. He has also written and directed over twenty school musical productions, both in Victoria and New South Wales.

In his spare time Brian loves to garden, play golf, walk several fluffy dogs and write children's stories. Brian and his wife Robyn have been married for forty-six years and have three wonderful children, Adam, Jade and Tahla and the most amazing grandchildren, Luca, Lilly and Isla.

Printed in the United States
By Bookmasters